THE ISRAELI-PALESTINIAN CONFLICT

THE ISRAELI-PALESTINIAN CONFLICT

Other books in the At Issue series:

Affirmative Action
Anti-Semitism
Are Efforts to Reduce Terrorism Successful?
Club Drugs
Do Animals Have Rights?
Does the World Hate the United States?
Do Infectious Diseases Pose a Serious Threat?
Do Nuclear Weapons Pose a Serious Threat?
The Ethics of Capital Punishment
The Ethics of Euthanasia
The Ethics of Genetic Engineering
The Ethics of Human Cloning
Fast Food
Gay and Lesbian Families
Gay Marriage
Gene Therapy
How Can School Violence Be Prevented?
How Should America's Wilderness Be Managed?
Internet Piracy
Interracial Relationships
Is Air Pollution a Serious Threat to Health?
Is America Helping Afghanistan?
Is Gun Ownership a Right?
Is North Korea a Global Threat?
Is Racism a Serious Problem?
Is There Life After Death?
Media Bias
The Peace Movement
Private Character and Public Office
Reproductive Technology
Sex Education
Should Juveniles Be Tried as Adults?
Should the United States Withdraw from Iraq?
Teen Suicide
Treating the Mentally Ill
UFOs
Women in the Military

THE ISRAELI-PALESTINIAN CONFLICT

John Boaz, *Book Editor*

Bruce Glassman, *Vice President*
Bonnie Szumski, *Publisher*
Helen Cothran, *Managing Editor*

GREENHAVEN
PRESS ®

San Diego • Detroit • New York • San Francisco • Cleveland
New Haven, Conn. • Waterville, Maine • London • Munich

© 2005 by Greenhaven Press. Greenhaven Press is an imprint of Thomson Gale, a part of the Thomson Corporation.

Thomson is a trademark and Gale [and Greenhaven Press] are registered trademarks used herein under license.

For more information, contact
Greenhaven Press
27500 Drake Rd.
Farmington Hills, MI 48331-3535
Or you can visit our Internet site at http://www.gale.com

LIBRARY OF CONGRESS CATALOGING-IN-PUBLICATION DATA

The Israeli-Palestinian conflict / John Boaz, book editor.
   p. cm. — (At issue)
Includes bibliographical references and index.
ISBN 0-7377-1981-8 (lib. : alk. paper) — ISBN 0-7377-1982-6 (pbk. : alk. paper)
   1. Arab-Israeli conflict. 2. Palestine—Politics and government—1948– . I. Boaz, John. II. At issue (San Diego, Calif.)
DS119.7.I82685 2005
956.9405—dc22
                                                  2004040526

Printed in the United States of America

Contents

Introduction

In late March 2002 a suicide bomber blew himself up in a hotel in the town of Netanya in Israel, killing himself and twenty others. More than 130 people were injured in the blast. The bomber was discovered to have been a member of the Islamic Resistance Movement, or Hamas, a group of radical Islamic fundamentalists opposed to the existence of Israel in any form. Although suicide bombings are not uncommon in Israel, the Netanya hotel bombing was significant for two reasons: One, it occurred during the sacred Jewish holiday of Passover, and so appeared to be a direct assault not only on Jewish civilians but also on the very fabric of Jewish culture; and two, the bombing came just days after the unveiling of an Israeli-Palestinian peace plan drafted by Crown Prince Abdullah of Saudi Arabia, which sought to end the long-standing Middle East conflict. This pattern of terrorist attacks abruptly putting an end to peace talks has long characterized the Israeli-Palestinian Conflict. Another entrenched pattern central to the conflict is military reprisals following terrorist attacks.

Indeed, Israeli prime minister Ariel Sharon responded to the Netanya bombing by saying that "Israel will act to crush the Palestinian terrorist infrastructure, in all its parts and components." Shortly thereafter, the Israeli Defense Force (IDF) launched Operation Defensive Shield, which attacked suspected terrorist targets in occupied Palestinian territories and isolated Palestinian Authority president Yasir Arafat at his compound in Ramallah. The Passover massacre, as the Netanya hotel bombing came to be known, seemed designed to thwart any efforts at ending the decades-old Israeli-Palestinian conflict, which had gained renewed significance on the world stage in the wake of the terrorist attacks on the United States on September 11, 2001.

After the September 11 attacks, the United States embarked on a war against terrorism, pressuring its allies to aid in the effort. Israel responded by renewing its commitment to retaliate against Palestinian terrorist attacks. As Prime Minister Sharon noted in the days following the September 11 tragedy, soldiers in the war on terrorism "must fight against all terrorist organizations, including those belonging to Arafat" as well as "Islamic Jihad, Hamas, and Hizbullah," all Islamic fundamentalist organizations that have carried out terrorist attacks against Israel. This imperative to halt terrorism at all costs has significantly escalated the conflict in the form of Israeli crackdowns on Palestinian "terrorists." Predictably, these Israeli reprisals have been followed by new Palestinian terrorist attacks, which in turn provoke an ever-increasing military response from Israel.

Terrorism, defined by the U.S. State Department as "premeditated, politically motivated violence perpetrated against noncombatant targets," has always been a factor in the Israeli-Palestinian conflict, even before Israel officially became a sovereign nation in 1947. Pogroms, or race riots in which Jews were massacred, were common in the Middle East in the 1920s and 1930s. The most vicious of these attacks occurred in 1929 in the town of Hebron, the oldest Jewish community in the world. Arab rioters killed nearly 10 percent of the town's Jewish population, and the remaining inhabitants were forced to flee. Israel did not regain Hebron until after the Six-Day War against Jordan, Syria, and Egypt in 1967. To counter the threat of continued violence, Jews formed several paramilitary groups, which could be classified as terrorist groups since they attacked civilian targets to achieve political ends.

Although the Israeli government dismantled or absorbed its paramilitary units after the creation of the state of Israel, the number of Palestinian and Islamic fundamentalist terrorist groups has increased during the decades of conflict. Islamic Jihad and Hamas are but two examples of militant groups that consistently carry out terrorist attacks against Israeli civilians. Many analysts have also labeled the Palestinian Liberation Organization (PLO) a terrorist group.

Popular uprisings among the Palestinian people have been aided by these terrorist groups. In December 1987, Palestinians in the West Bank and Gaza rose up in a popular civil revolt or intifada. By early 1988, it was clear that the PLO was helping to coordinate many of the intifada's actions, including the creation of large mobs, the stoning of Israeli cars, and attacks against Israeli civilians. A second, much more violent and deadly intifada began in September 2000. Terrorists started to use suicide bombing with increased frequency in order to advance their goal of liberating Palestine. In this hostile climate, Israel and Palestine have faced the daunting task of seeking a peaceful solution to their conflict.

Several peace initiatives have been proposed throughout the Israeli-Palestinian conflict, and all of them have met with varying degrees of success and failure. U.S. president Jimmy Carter brokered the Camp David Accords between Israel and Egypt in 1978 and 1979. This agreement stabilized the Middle East slightly and provided a framework for establishing Palestinian autonomy. Although Israel followed through on its promised concessions to Egypt, the Palestinians would not allow Egyptian president Anwar Sadat to negotiate on their behalf, and the Palestinian provisions of the accords were not implemented. Following the failure of Camp David, violence between the Israelis and Palestinians continued.

Over a decade later, in 1993, secret talks were held between the Israeli government and the Palestinian Authority in Oslo, Norway. Although both Palestinians and Israelis made several concessions for peace, the talks collapsed when a Jewish extremist, Baruch Goldstein, opened fire on a group of Muslim worshippers in Hebron at the Tomb of the Patriarchs, a major Muslim shrine. In 2000 peace talks again collapsed when Yasir Arafat walked away from negotiations at Camp David and Taba, Egypt, because he felt that the concessions offered by the Israelis and the Americans did not go far enough in achieving Palestinian goals of sovereignty and self-determination.

All of these peace plans have crumbled in part because of the cycle of terrorist attacks followed by increasingly severe reprisals. Terrorist attacks like the Passover massacre and military reprisals like the assault on the Jenin refugee camp would be the norm well into 2003, ensuring that any peace proposal was almost guaranteed to fail. The situation has understandably inspired many U.S. presidents and other world leaders to embark on efforts to resolve the conflict. President George W. Bush said in a policy speech on June 24, 2002, that "it is untenable for Israeli citizens to live in terror. It is untenable for Palestinians to live in squalor and occupation. And the current situation offers no prospect that life will improve." He added, "If all parties will break with the past and set out on a new path, we can overcome the darkness with the light of hope."

Despite the efforts of the United States, Israel, the Palestinian Authority, and other nations, all attempts so far to bring about an end to the conflict have failed. The 2003 U.S.-backed "road map to peace," which contained as a prerequisite for peace the immediate cessation of terrorist attacks against Israel, is just the latest example of a failed peace plan. It stalled when the former Palestinian prime minister, Mahmoud Abbas, and his successor, Ahmed Queri, were unable to halt the terrorist activities of Islamic militant groups. Indeed, with dreary regularity, violence between the parties generates new peace plans, and violence inevitably derails them.

Although the events of September 11 prompted renewed efforts to resolve the Israeli-Palestinian conflict as a major step in fighting the global war on terror, conditions in the region have effectively thwarted any real steps toward peace. The articles in *At Issue: The Israeli-Palestinian Conflict* provide opinions on the various causes of and possible solutions to the Israeli-Palestinian conflict in the context of a post–September 11 world.

1

Israel Is to Blame for the Israeli-Palestinian Conflict

Alphonse De Valk

Alphonse De Valk is editor of the magazine Catholic Insight.

The present-day hostilities between Israelis and Palestinians can be traced to the Six-Day War of 1967. Following Israel's success in this war against the Arab states, the Israeli government decided to occupy the territories of and establish colonies in the Golan Heights, the West Bank, and the Gaza Strip. Palestinians in these territories were stripped of their rights and privileges, and Israel has been unwilling to allow the formation of an independent Palestinian state that might satisfy Palestinian demands for redress. It is up to Israel to end the Israeli-Palestinian conflict by surrendering its settlements to the Palestinians.

First, let us exclude considerations of religion and history. While it may be interesting to go back to the Old Testament and God's promise to Moses, or review the history of Muhammad and Muslim conquests, or study Theodore Herzl [founder of the Zionist movement] and the birth of Zionism around 1900, it is not really all that useful. History is obviously relevant because it bears on many decisions that people make, certainly in the case of the creation of Israel as a separate state in 1948. But history does not explain what people will do in the future.

The events that govern today's situation occurred in 1967 when Israel, after defeating the armies of the Arab states, made a two-fold judgment. Its leaders decided, first, that the territories called the Golan Heights, the West Bank and the Gaza Strip should be retained for state security reasons; and, secondly, that they should get Jewish families to settle among the existing Arab population in separate settlements. The second decision, especially, was hotly debated at the time. Some of Israel's leaders opposed it, warning that it would endanger Israel itself. Their prophecies have come to pass.

Once the decision to build Jewish settlements was put into action, the territories added to Israel began to look step-by-step like "occupied" territories, and the Israeli Defence Force (IDF) began to turn into the Israeli Occupation Force. Israel's course of action, moreover, was made contrary to the will and the resolve of the United Nations, and was supported only by the United States, whose powerful Israeli lobby dominates [U.S.] Middle East foreign policy. The American veto in the Security Council and on the ground ensured that all further UN resolutions remained ineffective.

Conditions in the Territories

Within the Territories, acts of injustice against the Arab population became daily occurrences. The City of Jerusalem expropriated West Bank land on a large scale. Land also was taken elsewhere, orchards plowed under and houses demolished as the settlements grew to 200 by 1992. These wanted their own roads, first to Israel itself and then to other nearby settlements so as to form a communications grid.

Once the decision to build Jewish settlements was put into action, the territories added to Israel began to look step-by-step like "occupied" territories.

Meanwhile, two million Arabs living in "the Territories" in 1967 (3.4 million [as of April 2002]) had no rights. Entry into Israel for finding work was turned on and off like a water tap; their educational institutions were closed regularly for infractions of this or that law; political, educational, commercial and social institutes were impossible to develop; personal humiliations with curfews, travel bans, arrests, beatings and imprisonment were encountered daily, while Israeli police agents were busily bribing poverty-stricken families to inform on resisting neighbours.

As for the one million Arabs who live within Israel itself and who have acquired Israeli citizenship, they too are only third-rate Israelites. They cannot own property outside their original small enclaves; they cannot buy homes to live anywhere in Israel; they may not serve in the Israeli army; and they find themselves constantly discriminated against in applying for jobs, especially state-controlled jobs.

Failed attempts at solutions

By 1992, it was clear to most observers of Palestinian affairs that something needed to be done. There followed the Oslo agreements,[1] which for the first time held out hope for a new beginning. Arab self-determination was recognized by the Israelis in return for a formal acknowledgement of Israel's right to exist. The rest of the world was to invest in Palestinian enterprise and help them build political institutions (the Palestinian Authority), with a state apparatus of administration, police, registrations, etc. Israel was to halt any increase in settlements. Above all, there was to be dialogue and consultations for further developments.

The above initiatives were realized in the years following 1992. The

1. Peace accords negotiated in Oslo, Norway, between the Palestinian Authority and Israeli officials.

police were provided with light arms. Yasser Arafat was installed as head of the [Palestinian] government. Everything seemed to move forward as it should, except for one thing: succeeding Israeli prime ministers and their cabinets could not reconcile themselves to the idea of a truly autonomous Palestinian state. The "facts on the ground," that is, the Jewish settlements in "the Territories," did exactly what the late prime minister Menachem Begin, who had started them, had foreseen they would. They made the surrender of the West Bank and Gaza unpalatable. While not increasing the number of settlements as agreed in Oslo, Israel doubled them in size from 100,000 inhabitants to 200,000 over a five-year period (1993–98), thus revealing its true plan: it had no intention of allowing a Palestinian state.

That is where we are today. [Israeli] Prime Minister Ariel Sharon, a bitter opponent of Oslo, has added 34 new settlements in 2001 alone. Was Israel duplicitous in its dealing with the Palestinians? Perhaps yes, perhaps no. The "facts on the ground" begun in 1968 may have gradually crept up in their consciousness, and now their hands are tied.

At any rate, the future seems clear enough. The Arab nations have offered to fully recognize Israel as a legitimate entity in the Middle East. That offer should be accepted. In return, Israel should surrender their "settlements" to the Palestinians and allow a new state to develop. The United States, Europe and Canada should guarantee Israel's security.

Impossible, you say, in today's climate? My answer: there is no other solution which will bring peace with justice.

2

Palestinians Are to Blame for the Israeli-Palestinian Conflict

Leon Wieseltier

Leon Wieseltier is the literary editor of the New Republic.

Although the Israeli-Palestinian conflict has been under way for several decades, it is only since the second intifada, or Palestinian uprising, that the fight has escalated to the status of a full-scale war. When Palestinian leader Yasir Arafat refused the peace process advocated by the Clinton administration in 2000, he knowingly chose the horror of war for the Palestinian people. The Palestinians have demonstrated through their terrorist tactics and their constant refusal to honor calls for cease-fires that they prefer passion over politics, struggle over solution. It is the constant Palestinian attacks against Israelis coupled with the belief that such attacks will further the Palestinian cause that points to the Palestinians as the source of the conflict.

The Arab-Israeli conflict is over half a century old, and the struggle over the precious, punishing land between the river and the sea is over a century old, but what we are now witnessing, with perfectly appropriate horror, is the first Palestinian-Israeli war. It is, in important respects, an asymmetrical war. Israel is a state and Palestine is a proto-state; Israel has a powerful military machine and Palestine has a powerful terror machine. But on the battlefield of legitimacy, of the right to statehood in this particular place, the Israelis and the Palestinians are evenly matched; and the relative military weakness of the Palestinians has not prevented them from sending an unprecedented shudder through Israeli society, and from committing unspeakable crimes. The Palestinians also possess a variety of military organizations: The savage campaign of Palestinian terror is only a part of the armed resistance to the Israeli occupation that is the real innovation of these terrible days. For the first time since the creation of Israel [in 1948], the Palestinians are fighting for a Palestine in Palestine.

They have understood what Israel grasped a long time ago: that all the Arab-Israeli wars were fought by the Arab states not for Palestine but against Israel. This accounts for the strange exhilaration that the Palestinians express about their own tribulations, for the spirit of apocalypse in which they are acting, for the costly illusion that they are attaining something by war that they could not have attained by peace.

Instead of Palestinian diplomacy there is Palestinian delirium.

As of [April 2002], 1,229 Palestinians and 408 Israelis have perished in this war. The disparity between those awful numbers is a reflection of the military superiority of Israel, and also of the political folly of the Palestinians. If it is the sovereign state of Palestine that they want, they could have gained it more than once without the tears. The Palestinians are mounting armed resistance against an occupying power that for a quarter of a century has been divesting itself of territories that it is occupying, except not in a manner that will damage it or destroy it. To be sure, there are Israelis who believe that the return of any of the territories would damage or destroy Israel; but those Israelis have failed to persuade the majority of their countrymen that their pessimism or their jingoism is correct. It is the fears of the Jewish settlers that have a basis in reality: not only because they now find themselves in an extraordinarily perilous position (even [Israeli prime minister] Ariel Sharon proposed a security buffer that would have left them on the insecure side), but also because they have recognized that they are not the obstacle to a diplomatic solution that they planned to be. In [the American presidential retreat] Camp David in 2000, these outposts of piety and vulnerability were no impediment at all; the negotiations broke down over the Palestinian right of return, when Palestinian leaders again shirked the choice between their desire for a state and their desire for their grandfather's house. And a few days after the suicide bombing in Netanya, after the slaughter that made that night different from all other nights, [the Israeli newspaper] *Yediot Aharonot* published a poll that reported 66 percent of the Israelis supporting the dismantling of all the settlements in Gaza and 70 percent supporting the dismantling of settlements in populated Palestinian areas. No, this Palestinian war for Palestine is a gratuitous war. Those 1,637 deaths are the direct consequence of [Palestinian leader] Yasir Arafat's cowardly decision to leave Palestine in his cabin at Camp David. He chose this.

Passion over politics

Instead of Palestinian diplomacy there is Palestinian delirium. This people that demands sovereignty is utterly without sovereignty over its passions. It prizes its passions more than it prizes any politics. It regards a cease-fire, a respite from the carnage that would make possible a resumption of negotiations, as a defeat. It is acting on a doctrine that might be called strategic death. The suicide bombers (who would be known more precisely as homicide bombers, but for the fascination that such perversion provokes) believe that death is a strategy for winning a passage to heaven. Their masters in [the Islamic resistance movement] Hamas believe that death is a strategy for driving the Israelis out of the territories and maybe even out of the Middle East. Jews "love life more than other people," a senior Hamas official told Lee Hockstader of *The Washington Post,* "and they prefer not to die." The love of life he regards as a weakness. In recent weeks the internecine struggle between Palestinian secularists and Palestinian theocrats seems to have been resolved: the radicals of [Yasir Arafat's political movement] Fatah, the revolutionaries who defiantly preferred manifestos to surahs [chapters of the Islamic holy book the Koran], have also taken up the techniques of suicide bombing. They are all jihadists [holy warriors] now. The methods of Hamas were adopted by Fatah for the most chilling reason. They discovered that it was necessary to retain their political credibility. They pander to their people not by establishing schools and clinics. They pander to their people by blowing themselves to bits.

> *The Palestinians understandably wish to determine their own lives, but nobody ever built a life out of the hatred of life.*

The revered Palestinian poet Mahmoud Darwish was visited at the end of March [2002] by a delegation from the International Parliament of Writers, who came to express their solidarity with the Palestinians. When they asked him why he does not write about the present conflagration, Darwish replied: "I know that the masters of words have no need for rhetoric before the eloquence of blood." He then proceeded to deliver the usual writerly sermon that "our task, as humans, is to humanize history"; but the moral comeliness of the master of words was rather compromised by that single sickening sentence, by his agreement that there is beauty in murder. "The eloquence of blood": Whatever else such a locution is, it is a treason against literature. (The writers also visited Yasir Arafat in Ramallah, where Jose Saramago declared that "though there are differences of time and place, what is happening here is a crime that may be compared to Auschwitz. They are turning this place into a concentration camp." If this is Auschwitz, an Israeli reporter asked, where are the gas chambers? Saramago replied: "There aren't any yet.")

There is more, much more. In *Time* magazine [in April 2002], a Palestinian psychiatrist published an explanation of this mass hatred of life, sweetly called "Why We Blow Ourselves Up." It is one of the most twisted things that I have ever read. The doctor wishes to show why the collapse of reason is reasonable. "Ours is a nation of anger and defiance," he instructs. "The struggle today is how not to become a suicide bomber." He remarks, without a syllable of alarm, upon "a desire for revenge that every Arab harbors." He cites the Koranic promise of eternal life in paradise to those who sacrifice themselves for Islam, and comments that "Muslims, men and women, even secularists, hold to the promise literally." With clinical authority he maintains that "in every case of martyrdom there is a personal story of tragedy and trauma." This psychological alibi is then buttressed by an affecting anecdote: "A curious journalist once asked me to introduce him to a potential martyr. When the journalist asked, 'Why would you do it?' he was told, 'Would you fight for your country or not? Of course you would. You would be respected in your country as a brave man, and I would be remembered as a martyr.'"

The doctor is sick. His explanation is itself a clinical document. Anger is not a great human accomplishment, even when it is a condign response to events. All Muslims do not take the fairy tales of religion literally. Does every Arab harbor a desire for revenge? Then the Israeli right is right and there is no hope. Also there is a difference between heroism and martyrdom. A hero is somebody who risks everything for what he believes. A martyr is somebody who risks nothing for what he believes, because he believes that his reward is certain, and that his life really begins with his death. Martyrdom, unlike heroism, is an extreme and repugnantly rigid expression of certainty. Martyrs make dogmas, heroes make wagers. But here is Arafat in Ramallah, raving on al-jazeera [a Middle East news source] that he wishes to die like a martyr. Since he returned from the Catocin Mountains with nothing for his people except an interest in street battles, the chairman of the Palestinian Authority has resorted frequently to the theological vocabulary of holy dying. Surely the aspiring martyr cannot be relied upon to restrain the other aspiring martyrs. In truth, martyrdom is nothing but the sanctification of failure. It transforms losing into winning, so as to make winning—in this instance, the victory of a normal life in a state alongside another state with a normal life—seem like a surrender, a betrayal, a concession to the evil world. The martyrs of Islam resist the evil of the world by adding to its evil.

Middle-class Israel and resistance

The Palestinians understandably wish to determine their own lives, but nobody ever built a life out of the hatred of life. Moreover, the love of life is not a failing. It is the source of an ennobling ferocity. Happiness can make people strong. If Hamas believes that Israelis love life too much to fight for it, then Hamas is making a spectacular mistake. Israelis may not want to die . . . but they will not have the streets of Jerusalem and Tel Aviv and Haifa and Netanya stained with their own blood. Israelis can find a way to settle with the Palestinian fight for Palestine, but they cannot find a way to settle with the Palestinian fight against Israel; and a great deal of the recent Palestinian violence is of the latter kind, animated by a fantasy of extirpating the Jewish state. Against that violence and that fantasy the Israelis will vehemently defend themselves.

The manic materialism of Israeli society in the 1990s did not disarm it. Quite the contrary. The support that Ariel Sharon has enjoyed in Israel . . . is not owed to a broad enthusiasm for a Greater Israel. It is owed only to the sense that he is a man of force and that this is a time for force. Sharon dreamed for a long time of becoming the prime minister of his country, but he never fulfilled his dream until Arafat fulfilled it for him. It was Arafat, and his preference of the "Al Aqsa intifada"[1] over the accom-

1. The al-Aqsa intifada is the Palestinian uprising that occurred after Israeli prime minister Ariel Sharon's visit to the Temple Mount, a location holy to Palestinians.

modation with [former Israeli prime minister] Ehud Barak, who brought
Sharon to power; and it is Arafat, and his complicity in the massacres of
the innocents, who keeps Sharon in power.

This nightmare cannot go on.

And that, too, Israel may eventually hold against Arafat. For Sharon
is weirdly devoid of a political imagination. He is just a big fist. He sees
only military problems and only military solutions. He is correct in his
view that terrorism is the immediate and intolerable threat (at the Arab
summit in Beirut [Lebanon], the president of Syria declared that there was
no significant difference between military targets and civilian targets,
that "[w]e cannot divide whether they are armed or not. It is a right to resist"), and that it must be met with vicious and overwhelming force. But
what then? When the infrastructure of Hamas and Islamic Jihad and the
Al Aqsa Martyrs Brigade and the Tanzim and Force 17 has been undone,
what then? The Palestinians in their multitudes and in their rights will
still be there, unannexable and (Jews, remember who we are!) unex-
pellable; and the Israelis in their multitudes and their rights will still wish
to exist in peace and in decency in their homeland.

The difficulties of diplomacy

Soon there will come a day, hard as it is to imagine while Palestinians det-
onate themselves at Israeli checkpoints and there is a siege in Manger
Square, when work will have to resume on the only moral and practical
answer that there has ever been to this question: partition, territorial
compromise, a two-state solution, the establishment of a Palestinian state
in most of the occupied territories with security arrangements in the Jordan Valley and identity arrangements in Jerusalem. Sharon's ancient hostility to peace agreements will make him unfit for such work. Anyway
there is no guarantee that the work will bear fruit: It has been tried before. Indeed, the present war is so heartbreaking not least because it feels
like it is occurring "after peace." So far the handshake on the White
House lawn has yielded crushingly little. But this nightmare cannot go
on. Well, no, it can go on; but it is a matter of the most solemn historical responsibility to try to stop it. Nobody should be asked to resign themselves to such excruciations, to call such torments a destiny. . . .
    It is an old conviction of radicals that the worse things get, the better.
The Palestinian radicals, secular and religious, share this conviction. It was
one of the great contributions of liberalism to demonstrate the cruelty of
such a view. But now those who would make the peace, or at least unmake
the war, must rely on the same belief. They, too, must hold that hell will
lead to heaven; or if not to heaven, then to a dispensation significantly
more humane than what is now to be found on this scorched ground. But
how different can the morning be from the night? The latest chimera is
the notion that the introduction of American troops will make the difference. In support of this notion, the barometrically interesting Thomas L.
Friedman observed in *The New York Times* that "Palestinians who use sui-

cide bombers to blow up Israelis at a Passover meal and then declare 'Just end the occupation and everything will be fine' are not believable." This is just another way of saying that no moral or political demands may be made of the Palestinians of the sort that may be made of the Israelis. The Palestinians, you see, are civilizationally disadvantaged. But surely they are not. Surely they may be expected to recognize what is wrong with suicide bombings, and more generally with historical action founded on rage and despair. There is no reason for foreign soldiers to spare the Palestinians the pangs of auto-emancipation. Otherwise no peace will ever be real. Otherwise the morning will be forever like the night.

3

The Arab States Want to See Israel Destroyed

Joel Singer

Joel Singer is a former legal adviser to the Israeli Ministry of Foreign Affairs. He was also one of the chief architects of the 1993 Oslo Accords, which attempted to negotiate peace between Israel and the Palestinians.

The Palestinian claim that Palestinian refugees have the right to return to their native land, which now constitutes Israel, is commonly regarded in the Middle East as a stepping-stone to solving the Israeli-Palestinian conflict. However, in reality, it is a ploy by the Arab states to destroy Israel by flooding it with hostile Palestinians. The notion of the "right of return" thwarts efforts to construct an independent state of Palestine, acknowledged worldwide to be the key in achieving peace between Israelis and Palestinians.

Following the Palestinian rejection of [former U.S. president Bill] Clinton's peace plan early in January [2001], the Palestinian leadership and some of their supporters have alleged that the only way to resolve the Palestinian refugee problem pursuant to international law is by allowing the refugees to exercise their purported "right of return" to Israel. This is a distorted, one-sided picture that is fundamentally flawed both legally and factually. International law is not on the Palestinians' side.

The Palestinian refugee problem is rooted in the 1948–49 Arab-Israeli War. In 1947, realising that the Jewish and Arab communities of Palestine could not live together in one state, the U.N. General Assembly adopted Resolution 181 (II), which recommended partitioning Palestine into two states—one Jewish and one Arab. While the Jews accepted this plan, the Arabs rejected it, claiming that all of Palestine belonged to them.

When Israel declared its independence in 1948, all Arab states attacked it in an attempt to prevent its creation. In the wake of this war, hundreds of thousands of Jewish refugees fled from Arab countries to Israel, and, at about the same time, between 600,000 and 750,000 Palestinians fled to Arab states from the portion of Palestine that is now Israel.

This population exchange mirrored far larger population movements

Joel Singer, "The Wrong Right: International Law and the Palestinian 'Right of Return,'" *American Bar Association Journal*, January 2001. Copyright © 2001 by the American Bar Association. Reproduced by permission of the publisher and the author.

following the end of World War II, which involved millions of Hindus and Muslims in India and Pakistan, as well as Poles, Germans and other nationalities in Central and East Europe. These population exchanges were resolved through the integration of all refugees into the host states. While Israel absorbed the Jewish refugees, the Arab states refused to allow such resettlement and integration of their Palestinian brethren, preferring instead to exploit the Palestinian refugees to serve their own political agendas.

The right of return is a myth

Palestinians often refer to the U.N. General Assembly's 1948 Resolution 194 (III), which called for permitting refugees to return to their "homes," as legal support for an alleged "right of return" to the Jewish state. Contrary to this assertion, however, Resolution 194 (III), like all other U.N. General Assembly resolutions, is nonbinding and not part of international law. Moreover, it was specifically rejected not only by Israel but also by all Arab states, which voted against it (because they found it insufficiently anti-Israeli).

Additionally, Resolution 194 (III) emphasised that refugees should be permitted back only if they wished to "live at peace with their neighbours." In fact, the Palestinian insistence on a "right of return" to the Jewish state has always been intertwined with the rejection of Palestine's partition into two states and the continued Palestinian aspiration to destroy Israel. Thus, the infamous PLO's [Palestine Liberation Organization] Palestinian Covenant of 1968, which adopted the destruction of the State of Israel and the liquidation of the "Zionist presence" in Palestine as its main goals, stated in its Article 9:

> "Armed struggle is the only way to liberate Palestine. Thus it is the overall strategy, not merely a tactical phase. The Palestinian Arab people assert their absolute determination and firm resolution to continue their armed struggle and to work for an armed popular revolution for the liberation of their country and their return to it."

This fundamental point should be understood clearly and without illusion: When supporters of the Palestinians speak of implementing their "right of return" to Israel, they are not speaking of peaceful accommodation with Israel; rather, they are using a well-understood code phrase for the destruction of Israel.

Indeed, the several hundred thousand Palestinian refugees who actually left the area that is now Israel have multiplied into more than 3.5 million people, most of whom are not refugees, but second- and third-generation descendants of the original refugees. The fact is that there are currently 23 Arab states and only one Jewish state, which now consists of 5 million Jews and 1 million Israeli Arabs.

If Israel opened its gates to an additional 3.5 million Palestinians, who account for more than half of the Palestinian people, it would quickly disappear and be transformed into the 24th Arab state.

During the decades that followed the adoption of the Covenant, the Palestinians continued to insist that any solution of the Palestinian problem must involve the destruction of Israel, validating former Israeli Foreign Minister Abba Eban's observation that the "Palestinians have never missed an opportunity to miss an opportunity." In 1993, however, the Palestine Liberation Organisation, acting as the representative of the Palestinian people, agreed in Oslo,[1] in the context of the Israeli-Palestinian Mutual Recognition Agreement, to provide several commitments to Israel.

They include:

• A PLO recognition of "the right of the State of Israel to exist in peace and security."

• A PLO acceptance of U.N. Security Council Resolution 242 and its companion resolution 338.

• A PLO undertaking to annul the Palestinian Covenant's provisions quoted above, together with all other similar provisions calling for Israel's destruction.

Not part of the Oslo Agreements

Accordingly, a continued Palestinian insistence on a "right of return" to Israel, apart from being built on originally questionable legal foundations, also is inconsistent with these very fundamental premises of the Oslo Agreements. First, the PLO agreed to relinquish its assertion that the Palestinians have the exclusive right to the historic Palestine and agreed to divide Palestine into two states—one Jewish and one Palestinian. For the Palestinians to now revive the demand that more than half of the Palestinian people have the right to immigrate to the Jewish state repudiates the spirit, if not the letter, of the Oslo Agreements.

Second, U.N. Resolutions 242 and 338, which the PLO accepted, are the only U.N. resolutions referenced in the Oslo Agreements. As such, these resolutions—but not U.N. General Assembly Resolution 194 (III)— are the single existing, agreed-upon basis for the Israeli-Palestinian permanent status negotiations (which cover, among other issues, the refugee problem). U.N. Resolution 242 affirms the necessity for "achieving a just settlement of the refugee problem," but, importantly, does not mention a "right of return" or any other specific solution as the mandated or preferred way to settle that problem.

If Israel opened its gates to an additional 3.5 million Palestinians, . . . it would quickly disappear and be transformed into the 24th Arab state.

Third, in 1998, after years of delays, and in the presence of the president of the United States, the PLO finally amended the Palestinian Covenant and formally annulled its articulated goal of destroying Israel through armed struggle and the implementation of a "right of return" to the Jewish state. A revived demand to return to Israel certainly casts doubt on the veracity of the PLO's annulment of the Palestinian Covenant.

---

1. the Oslo Agreements reached in Oslo, Norway, between the Israeli government and the Palestinian Authority

Alternatively, Palestinians sometimes assert that a Palestinian "right of return" exists independently of U.N. resolutions, pointing to a series of human rights conventions, such as the 1966 International Covenant on Civil and Political Rights, Article 12(4), which states: "No one shall be arbitrarily deprived of the right to enter into his own country." The fundamental flaw of this argument is that, after Israel and the PLO agreed to partition Palestine into two states—one Jewish and one Palestinian—the Palestinians cannot continue to argue that the Jewish state is the Palestinians' "own country" and that they therefore are entitled to return to it.

It is doubtful whether that aspect of the Oslo Agreements has been effectively communicated to the Palestinian people and really accepted by all of its leadership. Regrettably, the evidence strongly indicates that this illusion of seeking to destroy Israel in stages, culminating in its elimination by flooding it with millions of Palestinians, remains a goal of large segments of the Palestinian people.

At this critical time in the evolving relationship between Israel and the Palestinians, it is important that everyone understand the commitments and tradeoffs undertaken by the two sides in Oslo. There is one viable solution to the Palestinian refugee problem that is consistent with the two-state approach of the Oslo Agreements, provides a just resolution of the Palestinian refugee problem and does so without destroying the Jewish state.

This is a plan by which Palestinian refugees who wish to resettle in Palestine would do so in the Palestinian state to be created side-by-side with the Jewish state. This plan would require a major international financial effort, in which Israel will participate, to help Palestinian refugees settle permanently either in the Palestinian state or in the countries in which they currently reside, as well as to support such host countries in their rehabilitation efforts.

Most Israelis have already accepted the necessity of making far-reaching concessions to conclude an agreement with the Palestinians. When the Palestinians also come to terms with this necessity by finally accepting the commitments undertaken by the PLO on their behalf, and especially by abandoning their dream of destroying the Jewish state by having it overrun by millions of Palestinians, the Palestinian-Israeli dispute can be resolved.

4

The Arab States Want Peace Between Israel and Palestine

Marwan Muasher

Marwan Muasher is the foreign minister of Jordan.

The Arab states recognize not only the terrible humanitarian conditions created by the Israeli-Palestinian conflict but also the benefits of a lasting peace between Israel and Palestine for the entire region. To that end, the Arab states met in Beirut, Lebanon, in March 2002 and drafted a groundbreaking peace initiative. The iniative advocates peace between Israel and Palestine, seeks to normalize relations with Israel and recognizes Israel's right to exist, and attempts to find a workable solution to the problem of Palestinian refugees who have been displaced by the Israeli-Palestinian conflict. This goes beyond Arab propaganda and should be treated by Israel as a genuine attempt at diplomacy by the Arab states. The iniative should also be recognized as a serious offer of peace.

The security and humanitarian situation in the West Bank, Gaza and Israel has never been worse. The current year [2002] has witnessed a total breakdown of trust between the two sides, with an alarming hardening, indeed radicalization, of positions in both camps. This is not an atmosphere conducive to any attempts to resume the political process, or steps to create a new dynamic able to successfully resolve this longstanding conflict. Surprisingly, we are nonetheless witnessing serious efforts to deal with the root causes of the conflict for both sides, most of them being put forward from an unexpected quarter for the Israeli public—Arab states.

To the Israeli public, this might seem like a hopeless piece of Arab propaganda. I beg to differ. Let me outline the various steps that Arab states have taken since the beginning of this year to attempt a serious alternative to the bleak options that seem to exist only regarding the conflict. I suggest that the Arab initiative unanimously endorsed in Beirut [Lebanon] in March of this year is a very serious attempt to squarely face the needs of both sides, and to satisfactorily address them. Consider the language of the Arab initiative regarding Israeli needs:

Marwan Muasher, "The Arab Initiative and the Role of Arab Diplomacy," *Bitter Lemons*, vol. 25, November 2002. Copyright © 2002 by Bitter Lemons. Reproduced by permission.

• "Consider the Arab-Israeli conflict ended": For the first time, Arab states commit to a collective offer to end the conflict with Israel. This is probably one of the most important demands of the average Israeli citizen—the knowledge that the conflict is terminated, and that no further claims on Israel or its territory will be put forward by Arabs—all Arabs.

• "Enter into a peace agreement with Israel, and provide security for all states of the region": The security of Israel, according to this article, would be guaranteed through one collective peace agreement with full security provisions, and would be assured not only by neighboring Arab states, but by ALL Arab states, none excluded. This has always been a key Israeli demand. Despite Arab fears of Israel, brought about by Israel's occupation of parts of three Arab states, one cannot deny the existence of a genuine fear on part of the average Israeli regarding his or her own safety. The above article assures Israel that its security fears are understood, and will be addressed by all Arab states.

• "Establish normal relations with Israel": This signals full recognition of Israel and the establishment of normal relations, such as those between an Arab state and any other state in the world.

• "Achievement of a just solution to the Palestinian refugee problem TO BE AGREED UPON in accordance with UN General Assembly Resolution 194": For the first time, the Arab world commits itself to an AGREED solution to the refugee problem, thus addressing Israel's concern that the demographic character of the Jewish state not be threatened. To be sure, the initiative calls for achieving a just solution of the problem in accordance with UNGA Resolution 194, but it points out that the implementation of that resolution has to be agreed. The key point here is that Arabs understand well that the implementation has to be both fair and realistic, and certainly agreed upon. In other words, there is no possibility of a solution that will lead to the changing of the character of the Jewish state. Fortunately, there have been many suggested solutions, at Taba [a city on the Israeli-Egyptian border] and elsewhere between Palestinian and Israeli interlocutors that point to the possibility of reaching a pragmatic settlement to this problem.

It is true as well that the Arab initiative also addresses Arab needs: Israeli withdrawal from all Arab territories occupied in 1967, and the establishment of an independent Palestinian state, with East Jerusalem as its capital. But previous negotiations between Israel, Palestinians and other Arab states have shown that these goals are well within reach.

Arab resilience and diplomacy

These are powerful pledges by all Arab states which should not be ignored. To those who are skeptical of Arab intentions, let me point out a seldom-mentioned point. Notwithstanding all the violence of the past year, and the hardening of positions in the Arab world (as well as in Israel), not one Arab state has asked to withdraw its signature from the Arab initiative, though there were many opportunities to do so. The Arab initiative is proving its resilience day in, day out.

There has been another new and positive element despite this bleak environment: The emergence of a pro-active, pragmatic Arab diplomacy, led by three Arab states that are key to the conflict: Egypt, Saudi Arabia, and Jordan. One should not underestimate the positive contribution that Saudi Arabia has brought to the process. With their huge Arab and Islamic credentials, the Saudis have consistently signaled a willingness to play a very pro-active role in the process, bringing along with them the consent of most of the Arab and Islamic worlds. Here we should remember that Jordan and Egypt have already signed peace treaties with Israel. The involvement of Saudi Arabia, which does not have any territorial disputes with Israel, should not be underestimated.

Arab diplomacy has not stopped with the launching of the Arab initiative, however. Ever since President [George W.] Bush made his speech on June 4, 2001, committing the United States to a two-state solution in three years as a solution to the conflict, key Arab states have tirelessly worked with the US and the Quartet [the United States, the European Union, the United Nations, and Russia] to develop a realistic plan to see this vision implemented. It is a plan that fully realizes Israel's security needs, and deals with them. The plan should be strong enough to guarantee that children can board a bus for school without fear. It should also be strong enough to guarantee children under the age of five a life free of malnutrition. Jordan has made clear its opposition to suicide bombings on moral and political grounds. But while we understand the emphasis on security FIRST, it cannot be security ONLY. We need to give people hope that they will live free of occupation, and that their children will not only survive, but prosper as well.

> *Arab states are meeting the challenge of peace and are fully engaged.*

The road map offers all that. It outlines a series of mutual commitments by both parties, targets to meet these commitments, and a monitoring and assessment mechanism by the Quartet to ensure that commitments are being fulfilled in time. To be sure, it is not perfect. All sides have reservations about parts of it, but it does have all the elements for a successful resolution of the conflict if it is adhered to, and accepted as a package. It does offer a tunnel, bumpy at times, but one that leads to light.

This road map should also lead to a successful conclusion not only on the Palestinian-Israeli track, but on the Syrian and Lebanese tracks as well. We do not view comprehensiveness as a concession to Arabs, as some have attempted to do. Comprehensiveness means the ability to trigger all the elements of the Arab initiative, in particular the ones I outlined above. We hope, therefore, that the three-year framework will apply to the Palestinian, Syrian, and Lebanese tracks with Israel in a way that can bring a permanent, comprehensive peace by mid-2005.

Optimistic, maybe, but certainly doable. Today, we have a clear international consensus on how to solve the conflict, going further than UNSC [UN Security Council] Resolution 242 did. It offers a two-state solution within a fixed time period, two elements missing from that famous resolution. More importantly, we have a willingness, and a contractual commitment, from all Arab states, to see an end to the longest conflict of the twentieth century.

There was a time when Israel accused Arabs of not stepping forward and providing a partner for peace. Today, Arab states are meeting the challenge of peace and are fully engaged. Let it not be said that they could not find a partner this time.

There is a way out, for both of us. There is an alternative that will allow all peoples of the region to live in peace, security and prosperity. But it will not be realized unless we both take a bold step forward. Let us do it together.

5

U.S. Aid to Israel Has Worsened the Israeli-Palestinian Conflict

Matt Bowles

Matt Bowles is a member of the organization SUSTAIN (Stop U.S. Tax-funded Aid to Israel Now!).

The oppressive Israeli military apparatus, largely responsible for the violence in Palestine, is heavily funded by the U.S. government and, consequently, by U.S. taxpayers. The amount of aid given to Israel is vastly out of proportion in comparison to other U.S. foreign-assistance endeavors and is actually in violation of American law, which stipulates that aid cannot be given to a nation that engages in a pattern of human rights violations. Israel's constant raids on the Palestinian population consistently violates Palestinians' human rights. Since it is clear that Israel will continue to violate Palestinians' rights, the only way to begin solving the Israeli-Palestinian conflict is to end all U.S. aid to Israel.

Israel has maintained an illegal occupation of the West Bank and Gaza Strip (Palestinian territories) for 35 years, entrenching an apartheid regime that looks remarkably like the former South African regime—hemming the Palestinians into small, noncontiguous bantustans, imposing 'closures' and 'curfews' to control where they go and when, while maintaining control over the natural resources, exploiting Palestinian labor, and prohibiting indigenous economic development.

The Israeli military (IDF)—the third or fourth most powerful military in the world—routinely uses tanks, Apache helicopter gunships, and F-16 fighter jets (all subsidized by the U.S.) against a population that has no military and none of the protective institutions of a modern state.

All of this, Israel tells its citizens and the international community, is for 'Israeli security'. The reality, not surprisingly, is that these policies have resulted in a drastic increase in attacks on Israel. These attacks are then used as a pretext for further Israeli incursions into Palestinian areas

Matt Bowles, "U.S. Aid: The Lifeblood of Occupation," www.leftturn.org, August 7, 2003. Copyright © 2003 by Left Turn. Reproduced by permission.

and more violations of Palestinian human rights—none of which makes Israeli civilians more secure; all of which further entrenches Israel's colonial apartheid regime. Most Americans do not realize the extent to which this is all funded by U.S. aid, nor do they understand the specific economic relationship the U.S. has with Israel and how that differs from other countries.

The aid pipeline

There are at least three ways in which aid to Israel is different from that of any other country. First, since 1982, U.S. aid to Israel has been transferred in one lump sum at the beginning of each fiscal year, which immediately begins to collect interest in U.S. banks. Aid that goes to other countries is disbursed throughout the year in quarterly installments.

Second, Israel is not required to account for specific purchases. Most countries receive aid for very specific purposes and must account for how it is spent. Israel is allowed to place U.S. aid into its general fund, effectively eliminating any distinctions between types of aid. Therefore, U.S. tax-payers are helping to fund an illegal occupation, the expansion of colonial-settlement projects, and gross human rights violations against the Palestinian civilian population.

A third difference is the sheer amount of aid the U.S. gives to Israel, unparalleled in the history of U.S. foreign policy. Israel usually receives roughly one third of the entire foreign aid budget, despite the fact that Israel comprises less than .001 of the world's population and already has one of the world's higher per capita incomes. In other words, Israel, a country of approximately 6 million people, is currently receiving more U.S. aid than all of Africa, Latin America and the Caribbean combined when you take out Egypt and Colombia.

This year [2003], the U.S. Congress approved $2.76 billion in its annual aid package for Israel. The total amount of direct U.S. aid to Israel has been constant, at around $3 billion (usually 60% military and 40% economic) per year for the last quarter century. A new plan was recently implemented to phase out all economic aid and provide corresponding increases in military aid by 2008. This year Israel is receiving $2.04 billion in military aid and $720 million in economic aid—these numbers will get more disproportionate each year until there is only military aid.

Most of this aid violates American laws.

In addition to nearly $3 billion in direct aid, Israel usually gets another $3 billion or so in indirect aid: military support from the defense budget, forgiven loans, and special grants. While some of the indirect aid is difficult to measure precisely, it is safe to say that Israel's total aid (direct and indirect) amounts to at least five billion dollars annually.

On top of all of this aid, a team from Israel's finance ministry is slated to meet with U.S. government officials . . . about an additional $800 million aid package which the Clinton administration promised Israel (and the Bush administration later froze) as compensation for the costs of its withdrawal from Lebanon. The U.S. also managed to find another $28 million in the 2001 Pentagon budget to give Israel to purchase 'counter terrorism equipment.'

According to the American-Israeli Cooperative Enterprise (AICE), from 1949–2001 the U.S. has given Israel a total of $94,966,300,000. The direct and indirect aid from this year should put the total U.S. aid to Israel since 1949 at over one hundred billion dollars. What is not widely known, however, is that most of this aid violates American laws. The Arms Export Control Act stipulates that U.S.-supplied weapons be used only "for legitimate self-defense."

Moreover, the U.S. Foreign Assistance Act prohibits military assistance to any country "which engages in a consistent pattern of gross violations of internationally recognized human rights." The Proxmire amendment bans military assistance to any government that refuses to sign the Nuclear Non-Proliferation Treaty and to allow inspection of its nuclear facilities, which Israel refuses to do. To understand why the U.S. spends this much money funding the brutal repression of a colonized people, it is necessary to examine the benefits for weapons manufacturers and, particularly, the role that Israel plays in the expansion and maintenance of U.S. imperialism.

Nature of the U.S.-Israeli relationship

In the fall of 1993, when many were supporting what they hoped would become a viable peace process, 78 senators wrote to former President Bill Clinton insisting that aid to Israel remain at current levels. Their reasons were the "massive procurement of sophisticated arms by Arab states." Yet the letter neglected to mention that 80% of those arms to Arab countries came from the U.S. itself.

Stephen Zunes (associate professor of politics at the University of San Francisco) has argued that the Aerospace Industry Association (AIA), which promotes these massive arms shipments, is even more influential in determining U.S. policy towards Israel than the notorious AIPAC (American Israel Public Affairs Committee) lobby. AIA has given two times more money to campaigns than all of the pro-Israel groups combined. Zunes asserts that the general thrust of U.S. policy would be pretty much the same even if AIPAC didn't exist: "We didn't need a pro-Indonesia lobby to support Indonesia in its savage repression of East Timor all these years."

The 'special relationship' between the U.S. and Israel must be understood within the overall American imperialist project and the quest for global hegemony, beginning in the late 1960s and early 1970s. For example, 99% of all U.S. aid to Israel came after 1967, despite the fact that Israel was relatively more vulnerable in earlier years (from 1948–1967). Not coincidentally, it was in 1967 that Israel won the Six Day War against several Arab countries, establishing itself as a regional superpower. Also, in the late 1960s and particularly in the early 1970s . . . , the U.S. was looking to establish 'spheres of influence'—regional superpowers in each significant area of the world to help the U.S. police them.

The primary U.S. interest in the Middle East is, and has always been, to maintain control of the oil in the region, primarily because this is the source of energy that supplies the industrial economies of Europe and Japan. The U.S. goal has been to insure that there is no indigenous threat to their domination of these energy resources. In the late 1960s and early 1970s, the U.S. made the strategic decision to ally itself with Israel and Iran, which were referred to as 'our two eyes in the middle east' and the 'guardians of the gulf.' It was at this point that aid increased drastically, from $24 million in 1967 (before the war), to $634 million in 1971, to a staggering $2.6 billion in 1974, where it has remained relatively consistent ever since.

Israel was to be a military stronghold, a client state, and a proxy army, protecting U.S. interests in the Middle East and throughout the world. Subsidized by the CIA, Israel served U.S. interests well beyond the immediate region, setting up dependable client regimes (usually military-based dictatorships) to control local societies. [MIT professor] Noam Chomsky has documented this extensively: Israel was the main force that established the Mobutu dictatorship in Zaire, for example. They also supported Idi Amin in Uganda, early on, as well as Haile Selasse in Ethopia, and Emperor Bokassa in the Central African Republic.

Israel became especially useful when the U.S. came under popular human rights pressure in the 1970s to stop supporting death squads and dictatorships in Latin America. The U.S. began to use Israel as a surrogate to continue its support. Chomsky documents how Israel established close relations with the neo-Nazi and military regimes of Argentina and Chile. Israel also supported genocidal attacks on the indigenous population of Guatemala, and sent arms to El Salvador and Honduras to support the contras [armed opponents of Nicaragua's government]. This was all a secondary role, however.

The primary role for Israel was to be the Sparta of the Middle East. During the Cold War, the U.S. especially needed Israel as a proxy army because direct intervention in the region was too dangerous, as the Soviets were allied with neighboring states. Over the last thirty years, the U.S. has pursued a two-track approach to dominating the region and its resources: It has turned Israel into a military outpost (now probably the most militarized society in the world) that is economically dependent on the U.S. while propping up corrupt Arab dictatorships such as those in Egypt, Jordan and Saudi Arabia. These regimes are afraid of their own people and, thus, are very insecure. Therefore, they are inclined to collaborate with the U.S. at any cost.

Prospects for activism

Since the end of the Cold War, the nuclear threat associated with direct intervention in the Middle East has disappeared and the U.S. has started a gradual and direct militarization of the region. This began with the Gulf War—putting U.S. military bases in Saudi Arabia (the primary source of oil), among other places—and has continued through the current 'war on terrorism.' This direct U.S. militarization has lessened the importance of Israel for U.S. domination of the region.

Although U.S. aid has not decreased yet, there have been other observable shifts. The first obvious one is the mainstream media reporting on the conflict. Although there is still, of course, an anti-Palestinian bias, the coverage has shifted significantly in comparison to ten years ago. This has been noticeable in both journalistic accounts of Israeli human rights abuses and the publication of pro-Palestinian op-eds in major papers such as the *Washington Post* and the *Boston Globe.*

There are also some stirrings in the U.S. Congress. Representative John Conyers (D-MI) requested that President [George W.] Bush investigate whether Israel's use of American F-16s is violating the Arms Export Control Act. Further, Senator Robert Byrd (D-WV) recently complained about giving aid without conditions: "There are no strings on the money. There is no requirement that the bloodshed abate before the funding is released." Other elected representatives are slowly starting to open up to the issue as well, but there is a long way to go on Capitol Hill.

Israel was to be a military stronghold, a client state, and a proxy army, protecting U.S. interests in the Middle East and throughout the world.

The most important development, however, has been the rising tide of concern and activism around the Palestinian issue in the U.S. left. The desperate plight of the Palestinians is gaining increasing prominence in the movement against Bush's 'war on terrorism,' and it is gradually entering into the movement against corporate globalization.

For years the Palestinian cause was marginalized by the left in America. Since this intifada [Palestinian uprising] broke out [in September of 2000], that began to shift significantly and has moved even further since [the September 11, 2001, terrorist attacks]. With the new 'anti-war' movement, there has come a deeper understanding of U.S. policy in the Middle East and how the question of Palestine fits into progressive organizing.

In Durban, South Africa [in September 2002], at the UN Global Conference Against Racism, one of the most pressing issues on the global agenda was the Palestinian struggle against Israel's racist policies. 30,000 people from South Africa and around the world demonstrated against Zionism, branding it as a form of apartheid no different than the system that blacks suffered through in South Africa. Shortly after, the U.S. and Israel stormed out of the conference.

In Europe and America, a range of organizations have risen in opposition to Israeli apartheid and in support of Palestinian human rights and self-determination. Just over the last year or two, organizations such as Students for Justice in Palestine, based at the University of California at Berkeley, have begun organizing a divestment campaign, modeled after the campaign that helped bring down South African apartheid. SUSTAIN (Stop U.S. Tax-funded Aid to Israel Now!) chapters in a number of cities have focused their efforts on stopping U.S. aid to Israel, which is the lifeblood of Israeli occupation and continued abuses of Palestinian rights.

Many Jewish organizations have emerged as well, such as Not in My Name, which counters the popular media assertion that all Jewish people blindly support the policies of the state of Israel. Jews Against the Occupation is another organization, which has taken a stand not only against the occupation, but also in support of the right of Palestinian refugees to return. These movements, and particularly their newfound connection with the larger anti-war, anti-imperialist, and anti-corporate globalization movements, are where the possibilities lie to advance the Palestinian struggle.

The hope for Palestine is in the internationalization of the struggle. The building of a massive, international movement against Israeli apartheid seems to be the most effective and promising form of resistance at this time. The demands must be that Israel comply with international law and implement the relevant UN resolutions. Specifically, it must recognize that all Palestinian refugees have the right to return, immediately end the occupation, and give all citizens of Israel equal treatment under the law.

We must demand that all U.S. aid to Israel be stopped until Israel complies with these demands. Only when the Palestinians are afforded their rights under international law, and are respected as human beings, can a genuine process of conflict resolution and healing begin. For all the hype over peace camps and dialogue initiatives, until the structural inequalities are dealt with, there will be no justice for Palestinians and, thus, no peace for Israel.

6

U.S. Aid to Israel Is Helping to Resolve the Israeli-Palestinian Conflict

American Israel Public Affairs Committee

The American Israel Public Affairs Committee (AIPAC) is a grassroots pro-Israel lobbying organization.

U.S. aid to Israel is a long-standing symbol of the special relationship between the United States and Israel, but, more importantly, it has positive effects on the Israeli-Palestinian conflict and on the Middle East in general. U.S. aid ensures that there is a stabilizing force in an otherwise completely unstable region and allows Israel to negotiate with its hostile Arab neighbors from a position of strength. Israel is more likely to seek a peaceful settlement with the Palestinians when backed by U.S. assistance. Moreover, U.S. aid supports the presence of a democratic government in the Middle East. Continued U.S. support of Israel is the best hope for peace and stability in the Middle East.

Aid to Israel is the single most tangible manifestation of the strength and immutability of the U.S.-Israel relationship. American assistance to Israel enhances U.S. national security by projecting American power and deterring potential aggressors without risking the lives of U.S. soldiers while supporting a reliable, front-line ally in our joint battle against weapons proliferation, terrorism and religious extremism. U.S. aid helps Israel maintain its qualitative edge over the combined militaries of its adversaries, thus allowing the Jewish state to consider taking risks—such as ceding territory—for peace.

Enhances U.S. national security

U.S. aid to Israel is an essential and efficient means of countering the biggest threats in the Middle East, including the proliferation of weapons of mass destruction; the use of terror to disrupt American-led peace mak-

American Israel Public Affairs Committee, "Aid to Israel," www.aipac.org, 2002. Copyright © 2002 by American Israel Public Affairs Committee. Reproduced by permission.

34

ing efforts; the potential disruption of access to Middle East oil; and efforts to impose strict Islamic sectarian government on the region.

The $2.64 billion in aid to Israel is highly cost-effective especially compared to the costs of deploying troops around the world. By comparison, the U.S. annually spends about $100 billion for NATO [North Atlantic Treaty Organization] defense in Europe and $50 billion in the Asia Pacific region, including $3 billion for maintaining 37,000 American troops in South Korea. Current U.S. expenditures in Iraq related to Operation Defensive Freedom are about $3–4 billion a month.

> *Virtually all U.S. aid to Israel—economic and military—helps Israel meet its security needs.*

By keeping Israel strong, U.S. aid helps deter would-be aggressors in the region without risking the lives of American soldiers. Israel has long served as a counterweight to countries such as Iran, Iraq and Syria—all of whom have a long history of provocation against their neighbors.

In short, Israel is a reliable, pro-American stabilizing force in an otherwise volatile region.

Promotes peace

U.S. aid enables Israel to negotiate from a position of strength. History has demonstrated that Israel is more likely to take historic steps for peace when it has full confidence in its key ally and supporter, the United States.

By ensuring that Israel can defend itself on the battlefield, U.S. aid helps encourage potential enemies to come to the negotiating table. The continuity of U.S aid sends a powerful signal to these adversaries that a negotiated settlement with Israel is the only option since the U.S. commitment to Israel is unwavering, regardless of which political party controls the White House or Congress.

Enhances Israel's security

Virtually all U.S. aid to Israel—economic and military—helps Israel meet its security needs. As other countries in the region enlarge and modernize their arsenals, this assistance gives Israel the means to obtain expensive, advanced American weaponry that it needs to defend itself.

U.S. aid reduces the risk of war in the Middle East by sustaining Israel's qualitative military advantage over the combined military forces of its adversaries who have an overwhelming numerical advantage.

By keeping Israel's army second to none in the region, this direct aid deters aggressors from attacking Israel without an American military presence, which Israel has never sought.

Without U.S. aid, Israel would lose the funding equivalent of nearly one-fourth of its defense budget.

Aid to Israel is one of the pillars of the U.S.-Israel strategic partnership designed to maintain stability in the Middle East. Other areas of cooperation include: cooperative weapons development, intelligence sharing, joint military exercises and military officer exchanges.

In keeping with an initiative by former [prime minister] Benjamin Netanyahu in 1996, Israel's overall aid package continues to decline. Israel's plan included the gradual elimination of its economic assistance package (ESF) while incrementally raising its military assistance (FMF) over a ten-year timeline.

Israel's aid appropriation for fiscal year 2002 is $2.64 billion, comprising $2.16 in military aid and $480 in economic aid. Of its military aid, approximately 3/4 is spent in the U.S.

Supports democratic ideals

The strongest allies of the U.S. are those countries that share our same values and democratic form of government. In a region dominated by authoritarian and military governments, Israel stands out as the only democratic country with regular, competitive elections, a free press and free speech.

Because of the special history of the U.S.-Israel relationship—and the proven strength of Israel's democracy—there is no doubt that the U.S. can depend on Israel in a crisis. In contrast, our relationships with other Middle Eastern countries are subject to unpredictable changes in policy and regime.

Israel is a steadfast ally that supports U.S. foreign policy and military actions, and votes with the U.S. at the UN more than any other country.

7

Only Israel's Withdrawal from Palestinian Lands Can Create Peace

Rashid I. Khalidi

Rashid I. Khalidi is a professor of Middle Eastern history at the University of Chicago.

The U.S.-backed "road map to peace" is flawed as an attempt to resolve the Israeli-Palestinian conflict because it neglects a key cause of volatility in the region: the Israeli occupation of Palestine. Neither Israel's military presence in the region, which Palestinians view as cruel and unacceptable oppression, nor the many Israeli settlements in Palestinian areas will be dismantled by the road map. The U.S. tendency to focus on Palestinian violence instead of on the Israeli occupation clouds the central issue of the conflict and guarantees the failure, in the long run, of the peace plan.

A pparently having learned nothing from the collapse of earlier efforts, the mainly American drafters of the road map included several features that almost guarantee its failure. One is the absence of a fixed timetable. Thus either party (in practice the Israelis, if the past is any indication) can hold up movement from stage to stage and within each stage. Another feature is the addition of interim phases to a process that is already prolonged. This means, in effect, the postponement of the most difficult aspect of the resolution of the conflict—the negotiation of issues like settlements, sovereignty, Jerusalem and refugees—until a third phase, which, if past practice is any guide, means indefinitely.

The theory of interim agreements, beloved of pro-Israeli "peace processors" in the Bush I and Clinton administrations, should have been buried for good by now, after the spectacular failure of the Madrid-Oslo[1] approach, which relied on such phased interim agreements. But this theory is resuscitated once more in the road map, in the form of a gratuitous

---

1. Peace negotiations held in Madrid, Spain, and Oslo, Norway, in the early 1990s.

proposal for "an independent Palestinian state with provisional borders and attributes of sovereignty." If the plan gets that far, this is a sure recipe for endless discord, which will be exploited by Israel to procrastinate further, while keeping the essentials of the military occupation and most Israeli settlements in business indefinitely, and restricting Palestinian control to as little of the occupied territories as possible—40 percent of the West Bank, if [Israeli prime minister] Ariel Sharon has his way.

"Washington is obsessively fixated on Palestinian violence as the root cause of all the problems between Palestinians and Israelis."

It is here that the road map is the most flawed. For in falling to focus on the Israeli occupation of the West Bank, Gaza Strip and East Jerusalem, about to enter its thirty-seventh year, and on Israeli settlements, which underpin that occupation, the road map misses an opportunity to end this conflict. Instead, it concentrates on Palestinian violence and how to combat it—as if it came out of nowhere, and as if, were it to be halted, the situation of occupation and settlement would be normal. This is a reflection of the preponderant US role in the drafting of this document. It is also a sign of why it will probably fail, for official "Washington is obsessively fixated on Palestinian violence as the root cause of all the problems between Palestinians and Israelis."

Problems caused by focusing on Palestinian violence

This obsession has led to an American focus on cosmetic changes in the Palestinian leadership, like the appointment of Mahmoud Abbas (Abu Mazen) as prime minister. His new government cannot possibly succeed in reducing Palestinian violence without a rollback of the tide of settlement and a release on the chokehold of the occupation. But that is unlikely to happen, for the [President George W.] Bush Administration's obsession with Palestinian violence to the exclusion of all else will probably lead to a continued bias in favor of the Sharon/Likud [Israel's conservative party] interpretation of the road map. By this interpretation, before Israel is required to do anything, the Palestinian security services, eviscerated by two years of pitiless Israeli attacks, must be reconstituted by Abu Mazen's choice to head them, Muhammad Dahlan, and then must wage a relentless war against the Palestinian factions that attack Israeli occupation forces and settlers in the occupied territories as well as civilians inside Israel. Palestinians complain that this means starting a Palestinian civil war before there is any indication that the Sharon government, dominated by hard-line supporters of the extension of settlements and the continued repression of the Palestinians, will do any of the things that are required of it. Nominally, the road map requires that both sides take steps simultaneously: Palestinian action against militant factions should take place alongside Israel's dismantling of settlements, and releasing its grip on the more than 3 million people of the occupied territories, who have lived for most of the past two years under siege, curfew and constant threat of Israeli attack.

But with the neocons [or "new conservatives"] riding high in Washington, with the Pentagon having taken over many of the responsibilities of the State Department and the CIA, and with the Bush Administration already in campaign mode and the Israeli lobby flexing its grotesquely well-developed muscles, there should be little doubt which interpretation of the road map will prevail in Washington. All that remains is to await precisely how this latest fledgling dove will turn into road kill, and what such a development will portend.

Should the Sharonistas who dominate the Bush Administration continue to prevail, as they have in nearly every Washington showdown since [the September 11, 2001, terrorist attacks], not only will this effort fail, as they and Sharon desire, but the Palestinians will be blamed for it. There will undoubtedly continue to be enough Palestinian violence to justify this, though it will pale alongside the routine, mechanized violence of the occupation. Beyond the daily brutality of a foreign army policing and denying the rights of a civilian population while their land is being stolen for the benefit of settlers, force has been used indiscriminately in heavily populated areas to crush Palestinian resistance, as per the words of Lieut. Gen. Moshe Ya'alon, the Israeli army chief of staff: "The Palestinians must be made to understand in the deepest recesses of their consciousness that they are a defeated people."

Israel can probably continue to rely on the existing American media double standard, whereby Palestinian civilians slaughtered in packed urban neighborhoods by battlefield weapons like heavy machine guns, helicopter gunship missiles and tank cannons are only "collateral damage" in the search to assassinate militants, and do not count as much as Israeli civilians slaughtered in Israeli cities by Palestinian suicide bombers, while the three-to-one ratio of Palestinians to Israelis killed (most on both sides being civilian) is constantly ignored. Thus, over one ten-day period, twenty Palestinians, mostly civilians, were killed, and went unnamed and unmourned in the US media, which instead focused on three Israelis killed in Tel Aviv by a suicide bomber.

In the long run, it will not be possible to oblige Palestinians to protect the expansion of settlements and the continuation of occupation, which is what the Oslo accords did; during the decade after negotiations began in 1991, the settler population more than doubled. If this is what the road map tries to do, it will fail. It remains to be seen if even a fair implementation of this profoundly flawed document can revive the vanishing prospects of a two-state solution, or if this has been rendered untenable by thirty-six years of relentless settlement and occupation dedicated to sabotaging the possibility of an independent Palestinian state in the West Bank, Gaza Strip and East Jerusalem. If so, Palestinians and Israelis will have to find a new means of living together peacefully in the same land, a prospect that daily seems ever more remote.

8

Only Israeli Military Might Can Create Peace with the Palestinians

Mortimer B. Zuckerman

Mortimer B. Zuckerman is the editor in chief of U.S. News & World Report.

The Palestinian Authority has shown itself to be nothing less than a terrorist organization; it has made little to no effort to stop the activities of known independent terrorist groups in Palestine and, in fact, may help or encourage terrorists. In order to stop Palestinian terrorism and to have some chance of bringing about peace in the region, the Israeli army must actively seek out the terrorists. A strong but passive Israel cannot triumph over Palestinian suicide bombers who are not afraid to die; the only solution is for the Israeli army to forcefully root out terrorist cells in the hope of dismantling the Palestinian terrorist apparatus so that the violence can end.

The Israeli-Palestinian conflict is no longer an argument over land. It is nothing less than a front line in the West's battle with terrorism. The peace process begun with such hope in Oslo[1] is a Humpty Dumpty that cannot be put together again for this simple reason: The terrorists that took over the Palestinian Authority—terrorists in [Yasir] Arafat's Fatah [an acronym for Arafat's political movement]—are now plainly indistinguishable from the fanatics in [the Islamic resistance movement] Hamas whose goal has always been the eradication of the State of Israel as a Jewish state. Indeed, in an interview with the *New York Times*, the Hamas leaders, who live prosperously in Gaza, gloated over the deaths of innocents from suicide bombings and expressed their open unity with Fatah.

Ordinary Palestinians in Ramallah and Bethlehem and other townships are enduring hardship and danger because their dreams of peace

---

1. A peace accord between Israel and the Palestinians was reached in Oslo, Norway, in 1993.

and rehabilitation have been betrayed by the duplicitous leadership of Yasser Arafat and the extremists he has encouraged.

The difference in the attitudes toward peace of the Israelis and the Palestinian leadership is dramatically exemplified by the frustrations of the American representative, Gen. Anthony Zinni, to get both sides to stop the killing. The Israelis agreed to Zinni's cease-fire plan. The Palestinians refused, except on terms that make it clear that the cease-fire would serve only to regroup and relaunch their terrorist attacks. But worse still, when Zinni arrived in the Middle East, the Israelis had hard intelligence that two suicide bombers were going to explode themselves in a major shopping center. Rather than take pre-emptive action that might have contributed to an atmosphere of confrontation—and that might have torpedoed Zinni's mission—the Israelis gave their intelligence to the Palestinian security forces under Jibril Rajoub. Instead of suppressing the terrorists, the PA [Palestinian Authority] passed this highly sensitive information to the terrorists to help them avoid capture by the Israelis. Fortunately, the Israelis still managed to stop these terrorists before they could do their evil work. But the Israelis were not so lucky with another terrorist: Using Israeli intelligence, the PA placed him in jail—not to detain him but to shelter him from the Israeli security services. He was released in enough time to blow up a cafe in Jerusalem.

PA terrorist activities

The only conclusion is that the basic operations of the PA have been turned over to those who advocate terrorism, such as the Tanzim and al-Aqsa martyr movements, and that these anarchists are directed, financed, and guided by Arafat himself. The Israelis have discovered written evidence of Arafat's direct involvement in arming the lethal al-Aqsa terrorist group, which has been responsible for so many suicide bombings in Israel.

The oversimplified criticism of the Israeli effort to root out the terrorists is that their infrastructure is inaccessibly inside the heads of thousands of young people who dream of being martyrs and will multiply under assault. The truth is that the terrorist infrastructure lies in a core group of several hundred terrorist leaders who teach their young how to assemble explosives and provide them with information on where the "enemy" can be found and how they can be killed. The PA has been unwilling to control or arrest this group but instead shelters them. Several hundred were found in Rajoub's compound and many in Arafat's compound.

All of this is of one piece. The PA never wanted just the West Bank and Gaza. Their maps show Palestine filling the entire territory covering all that is now Israel. Their emblems cover Israel with two rifles and a grenade. The Palestinian mantra is that the issue is really about Israeli occupation of lands that the Arabs lost in the 1967 war. This is just a blind. Why? Because under Oslo, the Israelis transferred administrative authority for 98 percent of the Palestinians to a Palestinian administration and even fitted them out with 40,000 armed police in the hopes that they would maintain their own security. Further, at Camp David and Taba, Israel offered to turn over 97 percent of the disputed territories plus the Arab neighborhoods of East Jerusalem to Palestinian sovereignty and a Palestinian state, only to have this offer to withdraw rejected. The Saudi plan, which would oblige Israel to go back to the 1967 borders, failed because it goes beyond United Nations Resolutions 242 and 338, the base of the Oslo agreement, which mandate that Israel should have secure and defensible borders. The 1967 borders are simply indefensible because they would leave Israel with a national depth as small as 8 miles between Haifa and Tel Aviv and would leave its only international airport highly vulnerable to mortar and other attacks.

The terrorist infrastructure lies in a core group of several hundred terrorist leaders who teach their young how to assemble explosives.

To assess PA intentions, it is relevant to remember that the Palestine Liberation Organization was formed in 1964—when the West Bank and Gaza were under Arab sovereignty; when there were no settlements on the West Bank, no access to the old city of Jerusalem nor to the holy places critical to Jewish history and identity. It was not the presence of Jews in these places that prompted the terrorist harassment and vicious antisemitism of the Palestinians back in those earlier days. It was antipathy to the very existence of Israel.

The significance of Oslo was its recognition that there were two nationalities with legitimate historical bases for asserting a right to occupation. It was a reasonable expectation after the concessions at Oslo that the moderates on both sides would be able to take the final step of the compromises required on but a small amount of land. Yet even after Oslo, there never was an extended time without terror and violence fomented by Arab extremists who refused to accept Israel's existence as a Jewish state and thus blocked the possibility of a two-state solution. And the terror and violence were not just aimed at Israelis. The Arabs who wanted to accept compromise and division were intimidated by their own radical brethren. As [former U.S. secretary of state] Henry Kissinger wrote, "The number of Palestinian leaders [who want peace in the Western sense] is minuscule. The fundamental schism is between those who want to bring about the destruction of Israel by continuing the present struggle, and those who believe that an agreement now would be a better . . . showdown later on."

The idea that the Palestinians will eventually destroy Israel inhabits what Fouad Ajami called the "dream palace of the Arabs." Now the Arabs believe they have the momentum to destroy Israel because of the undoubted impact of the suicide bombings. This is why it is critical for Israel to break the Palestinian delusion that terrorism will make the Jewish state go away.

Pre-emptive attack is the only solution

Israel has no choice but to root out the terrorists in their bases. It is impossible for Israeli security to catch up with every deluded young Palestinian fanatic willing to blow himself or herself up in a pizza parlor, a supermarket, at a bar mitzvah, a synagogue, or a school, or to spray machine gun fire at a wedding party. This is not happening in some distant place but right where the Israelis live their day-to-day lives. They are experiencing the equivalent of the [September 11, 2001] terrorist attacks virtually every single day—an existence that is intolerable for an open, democratic society. Israelis deserve the world's support and sympathy because their struggle is not just for their homeland, justified as it is, but also because they are fighting a new, horrific, and exploitative form of terrorism that menaces all civilized societies.

Israel has no choice but to root out the terrorists in their bases.

The new terrorism calls for a new policy, one already well articulated by U.S. Secretary of Defense Donald Rumsfeld. "We have no choice. . . . It is physically impossible to defend at every time in every location against every conceivable technique of terrorism," the secretary of defense said recently. "Therefore, if your goal is to stop it, you cannot stop it just by defense. You can only stop it by taking the battle to the terrorists where they are and going after them."

This is a policy of pre-emption because deterrence no longer works. Deterrence is based on the assumption that people are unwilling to die. Deterrence will not work when people have been so conditioned by a culture of hatred and religious fanaticism that they will commit suicide in order to kill innocent civilians. The only way to deal with this new phenomenon of suicide bombers, and make it clear this will not work, is to go after them before they get us. But this strategy of pre-emption against suicide and terrorism will have to replace a strategy of deterrence for the United States and for Israel.

This war is also a media war. Many journalists are impervious to the carnage that defines daily life in Israel. And they are too often inclined to make a moral equivalent of the terror and the civilized response to it—as if there were no moral distinctions between the arsonist and the firefighter; between deliberately targeting innocent civilians and inadvertently killing innocents while pursuing terrorists; as if it weren't the purpose of the Palestinians to kill as many innocent civilians as possible; as if the Palestinians had not danced in the streets after the World Trade Center bombings, while Israel went into mourning; as if Israel hasn't proposed a real territorial withdrawal and compromise while Arafat's maps include all of Israel; as if Israel wasn't an open democracy and the PA wasn't a corrupt, authoritarian regime; as if Israel is not practicing restraint; as if it is possible to eliminate terrorism without going after the sanctuaries that are the root of the terrorist challenge; as if Israel, unlike America, is not permitted to engage in simple self-defense and thus gets the support of the press only when it is a passive victim.

There has been, and still is, in Israel a majority who want a peaceful settlement—over 60 percent in recent polls. They understand it would include a large withdrawal from the territories, including the dismantling of a large number of settlements. But not as a surrender; not by submission; not under pressure from terrorist bombings. Surrender would only embolden the terrorists and their perverse, destructive goals: What would be next? Forcing the Israelis to flee to the sea?

America shares these concerns because these terrorists are the enemies of humanity. Today they arouse the Arab street. Tomorrow they will cause this street to send new disciples practicing this ritual of human slaughter to the West, to Europe and the United States. Terrorism did not end with the World Trade Center and Pentagon bombings and the rout of [the international terrorist organization] al Qaeda in Afghanistan [after September 11]. It remains a fundamental threat to civil society in Israel and a fundamental threat to civil society in America and the West.

In 1981 the Israelis destroyed the Iraqi nuclear reactor and were condemned by many around the world. In 1990, when the war with Iraq broke out, we found out how farsighted this policy was. In the future, Israel will be recognized for destroying a new but no less dangerous reactor, the Palestinian ritual of death and terror by suicide.

9

Establishing a Palestinian State Can End the Israeli-Palestinian Conflict

David C. Unger

David C. Unger is a member of the New York Times *editorial board.*

It is generally believed among the American, Israeli, and Palestinian governments that the formation of an independent Palestinian state is crucial to resolving the Israeli-Palestinian conflict, but the proper way to achieve this end is hotly debated. Many in the Israeli government argue for a security wall that would separate Israel and Palestine, along with the ousting of the president of the Palestinian Authority, Yasir Arafat, whom many Israeli authorities view as a terrorist. Palestinians flatly reject these proposals. However, given their grievances with one another Israelis and Palestinians must work toward some version of a two-state plan. Other solutions, such as the construction of a new state inhabited by both peoples or the continuation of the status quo, would only lead to more violence.

President George W. Bush has declared that America supports a future Palestinian state, but will not help create one until the Palestinian people elect "new and different" leaders "not compromised by terror." The desirability of such a leadership change is clear. But making it a precondition for diplomacy could condemn Israelis and Palestinians to years, if not decades, of further death and devastation. . . .

President Bush has already recognized the path that must eventually be followed. His vision of two states, one Israeli and one Palestinian, living side by side, despite all the obvious problems, provides the only workable framework for peace. Movement down that path can begin today, looking beyond [Palestinian Authority president Yasir] Arafat, but not waiting for his actual departure. . . .

David C. Unger, "Maps of War, Maps of Peace," *World Policy Journal*, Summer 2002, pp. 1–10. Copyright © 2002 by *World Policy Journal*. Reproduced by permission.

The inescapable logic of a two-state solution

Almost 10 million people, 5.5 million Jews and 4.5 million Palestinians (of whom a million are currently Israeli citizens), now live between the Jordan River and the Mediterranean Sea. Some Palestinians still dream of driving the Jews beyond, or even into, the sea. An extremist minority of Israelis dreams of driving the Palestinians beyond the Jordan. Those dreams are probably more popular on both sides since the latest violence erupted [in 2000]. But the moral and military costs of attempting to carry them out would be forbidding, and, one hopes, the outside world would not sit still for it. It is a prescription for endless war, not peace.

Other alternatives to a two-state solution are more respectable, but no more practical. Israel's Likud Party recently reaffirmed its opposition to the creation of any Palestinian state in the West Bank or Gaza Strip. That can only mean continued occupation or, to borrow the contemptuous term Arabs long applied to Israel, permitting some kind of Palestinian "entity" that falls short of the usual attributes of statehood. Indefinitely prolonged occupation would be a prescription for more terror, more death, more economic pain on both sides, further radicalization of Palestinian opinion, and a widening schism between Israel's demography and its democracy. The occupied territories have been in near continuous revolt since 1987, except for the period when the Oslo peace accords[1] seemed to be leading toward Palestinian statehood.

The entity-versus-state debate boils down to little more than hollow semantics. Israel's own interests require that any Palestinian administration have both the military means and the international responsibility for suppressing terrorism emanating from within its borders. An entity with those powers and responsibilities is, whatever one chooses to call it, a state. It was Arafat's failure to live up to those responsibilities, not his ambitions for statehood, that aborted Oslo.

> *The PLO's [Palestine Liberation Organization] embrace of a two-state solution makes it Israel's most plausible Palestinian negotiating partner.*

Another theoretically possible, but practically foreclosed, option is the creation of one state with two peoples, each enjoying equal legal and citizenship rights—the so-called binational secular state. This Western-sounding solution solves the central problem by denying it. It leaves no room for Israel as a Jewish state, a self-sufficient refuge from persecution, pogrom, and Holocaust. Centuries of tragedy have convinced the overwhelming majority of Jews, in Israel and elsewhere, that a Jewish state is a necessity for Jewish survival. Perhaps some day, an evolving Jewish national experience will make a binational secular state a more attractive idea. A very small minority of mostly secular, Westernized Israelis have long supported the idea of a binational secular state and some still do. But

---

1. reached in Oslo, Norway, in 1993 between the Palestinian Authority and the Israeli government

no major Israeli party endorses their views.

There has also been an important strand of Palestinian support through the years for a binational secular state. The Palestine Liberation Organization advocated it during the 1970s, though not very persuasively, given the PLO's lack of respect for anybody's legal or human rights and its general political opportunism.

But in the late 1980s, the PLO accepted U.N. Security Council Resolutions 242 and 338[2] and embraced the idea of partitioning Palestine into two separate national states along the pre-1967 lines. Arafat is now firmly identified with the idea of a specifically Palestinian state and so is the main Palestinian opposition party, Hamas. The difference is that Arafat continues to advocate Palestinian statehood within the parameters of a two-state solution. If he means that sincerely, he must support the reciprocal idea of Israel as a Jewish state, as he claims to do. The logic of such an acceptance bears directly on the issue of Palestinian refugees wishing to return to pre-1967 Israel.

The PLO's embrace of a two-state solution makes it Israel's most plausible Palestinian negotiating partner. . . . Unfortunately, Arafat's reembrace of terrorism since September 2000 has also rendered him an unacceptable negotiating partner in Israeli eyes. It is nearly impossible to imagine [Israeli prime minister Ariel] Sharon and Arafat sitting down with each other for productive negotiations. But it is unlikely that significantly more forthcoming leaders will soon emerge on either side. The existing leaderships, it must be acknowledged, accurately represent the hopes and fears of their constituents. If peace is to come any time soon, it will probably be necessary for these two leaders to learn how to accept and talk to each other again, if only to ratify and legitimate the compromises put forward by the international community.

Learning the lessons of Oslo

Moving forward toward a two-state solution means moving beyond the failures and disappointments of Oslo and building on its successes. Oslo's details are familiar, but an unhelpful mythology surrounds its demise. What needs to be understood is the continuing validity of its underlying logic and the disastrous consequences of its stretched-out timetable.

Oslo was, at the beginning, a plan by two sides that did not trust each other but recognized they had to deal with each other to achieve a mutually desired goal. That goal was a negotiated end to Israel's military rule over a rebellious Palestinian population in the occupied West Bank and Gaza Strip. In the mind of former Israeli prime minister Yitzhak Rabin, Oslo was not about generosity or idealism or a newly benign view of Yasir Arafat. It was a way of extricating Israeli soldiers from the physical, moral, and political hazards of occupation in the West Bank and Gaza by transferring the burden of pacifying the Palestinians and suppressing terrorism to a Palestinian police force. It was also a way of strengthening the Zionist democracy Rabin believed in by rebuilding Israel's solid Jewish majority within a slightly amended version of the pre-1967 boundaries. In the

---

2. The resolutions provide for recognition of borders between Israel and Palestine and implement Israel's withdrawal from occupied territories.

mind of Yasir Arafat, Oslo pointed the way toward achieving his lifelong dream of creating and leading a Palestinian state. It was also a means to reassert, with Israeli assistance, the political dominance of the exile-based PLO over the more locally based groups who had organized and led the first intifada [Palestinian uprising].

Amid the ruins of Oslo, it is important to recognize not only the utopian hopes, but the carefully designed safeguards, of the original plan. Oslo broke down not so much because the concept was fatally flawed, but because it was multiply abused. It failed to survive in part because it was never loved enough by the broad Israeli and Palestinian populations. It started out as a leaders' peace and never really became a peoples' peace. Thus episodes of terrorism on the one side and delay on the other were quickly cited by Oslo's political opponents as evidence that the deal was a dead end, a dangerous mistake, a betrayal of fundamental interests.

When Oslo ran into severe challenges, no powerful leader on either side had the will or the arguments to defend it. One of its two principal Israeli sponsors, Yitzhak Rabin, was assassinated, while the other, Shimon Peres, was politically marginalized. For three crucial years, Oslo was left in the custody of Benjamin Netanyahu, an Israeli leader who hated it. On the Palestinian side, the situation was even worse. Yasir Arafat never really rook responsibility for the commitments he had both explicitly and implicitly made. Rather than try to bring his people along, he remained silent while others incited violence. Then, increasingly, he turned to incitement himself.

[Arafat] is, at least for now, the only man with whom Israel can make peace, and it is in neither country's interest to pretend he isn't.

Rabin deliberately deferred his most politically difficult decisions—Jerusalem, settlements, and Palestinian refugees—to the final phase of Oslo to be concluded in five years' time. That is one major reason settlement building continued unabated during Oslo, as did construction of new Israeli neighborhoods in East Jerusalem. Israel claimed to be negotiating in good faith to remove the elements of occupation in the West Bank and Gaza. But, as Palestinians could see, it was simultaneously creating new ones.

Arafat accepted the five-year timetable because it allowed him to defer his most difficult political problems as well. He would not have to explain for now, to the refugee families that had always been central to his political constituency, that he would be obliged to negotiate away any realistic chance that most of them would be able to return to their homes in the 78 percent of historic Palestine that would remain under Israeli rule. Nor would he have to explain to the rest of the Arab world any agreement to accommodate a continued Israeli presence in the Muslim religious center of Jerusalem. And, most importantly, until these issues had been resolved, he would not have to declare an end to the conflict between Israel and the Palestinians.

In retrospect, it is clear that Arafat exploited these ambiguities to sustain hopes for an outcome beyond what Oslo promised, and that he authorized the assembly of a Palestinian arsenal that could be used to fight for these more ambitious goals by means Oslo itself expressly prohibited. It is not yet clear whether Arafat actually decided to wage that fight before the breakdown of the second Camp David summit meeting in July 2000. Neither is it clear whether he directly planned and launched the second intifada or merely threw his own forces behind it once it began. In the latter view, his paramount concern may have been to prevent his leadership being swept away on a wave of public anger over his corrupt administration of the West Bank and Gaza, and the failure of Oslo to bring an end to Israeli occupation and create a Palestinian state.

What is clear is that Arafat's behavior, especially since September 2000, has discredited Oslo and perhaps permanently destroyed his own credibility as a peace negotiator in Israeli eyes. He has plainly broken his promise to recognize and uphold Israel's security and combat terrorism. Even if he now agrees to renew that promise, few Israelis will trust him to keep it. President [George W.] Bush's call for a new Palestinian leadership points to one appealing solution to that problem. Yet it is not in America's or Israel's power to replace Arafat. He is, at least for now, the only man with whom Israel can make peace, and it is in neither country's interest to pretend he isn't.

Oslo reached its culmination, and near fruition, in the talks at Taba, Egypt, in January 2001, which built on proposals made by America's lame-duck president, Bill Clinton, several weeks earlier. There, many of the issues which had held up agreement at Camp David were worked out and some optimists felt a full agreement was only weeks away. But by then, popular Israeli faith in Oslo was shattered. The [former prime minister of Israel, Ehud] Barak government was only days from an election it was about to lose decisively. Bill Clinton was about to leave office. The Al Aksa intifada, and Yasir Arafat's violent embrace of it, helped catapult Ariel Sharon, who had always opposed Oslo, to Israeli leadership. It also strengthened radical forces in the Palestinian community who do not believe in peacefully negotiated solutions and whose demands for a final settlement stretch beyond Oslo's basic formula of two states separated by a redrawn version of the June 1967 borders.

Oslo was undone by its seemingly reasonable strategy of postponing fundamental political decisions. The PLO had opportunistically traded in terrorism for a seat at the Peace table, not really renounced it. And it never honestly told its people that negotiating a two-state solution would mean that millions of refugees would never be able to return to their ancestral homes. Israel, for its part, failed to acknowledge that negotiating in good faith with the Palestinians about the future of the West Bank and Gaza Strip required, at the very least, freezing all further building and expansion of settlements there. Instead, the number of settlers rose by more than 50 percent during the years of the Oslo negotiations from 1993 to 2000. Settlement building, which undermines Palestinians' hopes, cannot be morally or legally equated with terrorism, which destroys real lives, Israel's settlement policy was clearly permitted under Oslo. What must be noted, however, is that in the agreed-upon bargain of "land for peace," one side took unilateral liberties with the land, while the other took unilateral liberties with the peace.

Deadlock between Israel and Palestine

Repeatedly, the Sharon government has made clear to Washington and to everyone else that it is far more interested in extracting a cease-fire from the Palestinians than in recommitting Israel to the Oslo agenda. That attitude contributed to the failures of Gen. Anthony Zinni's two missions, in late 2001 and early [2002]. For their part, the Palestinians rejected any approach that did not clearly link a cease-fire to movement on Oslo. And with Palestinian suicide bombers rattling Israeli society, Arafat has shown little interest in a cease-fire, period. Undoubtedly he expected Israeli military retaliation, but he also expected the scenes of Palestinian civilians suffering and dying at the hands of Israeli troops to rally international support to the Palestinian cause.

Sharon, after being criticized by Washington for offering no formulas for peace, now talks about very long-term "interim" arrangements to be negotiated without Yasir Arafat at the table. The idea that any credible Palestinian leader could agree, nearly a decade after Oslo, to a new plan offering no more than limited autonomy over no more than half the West Bank, stretched out over another 15 to 20 years, seems absurd. But Sharon, whose thinking appears frozen in the pre-Oslo past, seems deadly serious.

Arafat, with his popularity among Palestinians again falling and America and Israel trying to write him out of the script, now seems to place his hopes in the Arab League peace plan. Except for the very important new element of Arab recognition, that plan sounds a lot like Oslo, in both its original concept and Taba details. If Sharon seems determined to forget that Oslo ever happened, Arafat seems equally determined to forget that it collapsed, and even though he played a substantial part in its breakdown, he has the more realistic view.

With these two leaders so far apart and frozen in their positions, the only way forward at this time is a concerted push from outside, led by the United States, starting as soon as possible. There is no guarantee that such an effort will succeed. But one new factor may help. Under the impact of a communications revolution that has brought satellite television images of West Bank clashes into every Arab city and village, the rulers of Saudi Arabia and Egypt seem slowly to be coming around to the view that the long-term stability of their own regimes depends on peacefully resolving the Israeli-Palestinian conflict. Arab leaders may be able to deliver changes in the Palestinian Authority and its negotiating positions, though probably not including the departure of Arafat. But only Washington can persuade Israel to take such changes seriously and return to the table. For that to happen. George W. Bush will have to commit the full power and prestige of his presidency to a determined new peacemaking effort.

In the absence of peace, separation may proceed. But there should be no mistaking it for peace. Peace will come only when Israelis and Palestinians have reached agreement on a two-state solution. We already know pretty much what that agreement will look like. What we don't know is how many more Israelis and Palestinians will die before it is achieved.

10

The Plan to Establish a Palestinian State Is Flawed

Eric L. Rozenman

Eric L. Rozenman is the former executive editor of International Jewish Monthly.

The two-state solution advocated by the United States to resolve the Israeli-Palestinian conflict, in which both Israel and Palestine would have sovereign, independent states, is seriously flawed. It assumes that the two states would be willing to recognize and accept the existence of the other, when it is uncertain that this is possible. Proposal of the two-state solution seems only to promote Palestinian nationalism and thereby to fan the flames of Palestinian terror. A strong Israeli state, large enough to be defensible, is required. Otherwise, the Jewish population in the Middle East will find itself at the whims of the Arab states. The Palestinians should be absorbed into one of the existing Arab states, such as Jordan, which is the only viable "two-state" solution.

The "two-state solution" to the Arab-Israeli conflict—actually a three-state solvent in which an irredentist Palestine, unstable itself, would destabilize Jordan and Israel—was stillborn in the 1970s. Renewed advocacy of it [in 2002] by "the quartet" of the United States, Russia, the European Union, and the United Nations prior to Palestinian reform and without realistic prospects thereof contradicted President [George W.] Bush's June 24 vision of a post-[Palestinian Authority president] Arafat, non-violent, democratic West Bank and Gaza Strip. Prime Minister Ariel Sharon's acceptance, albeit qualified, of a 23rd Arab country on soil he himself long considered Israel's strategic and national heartland confirmed a dangerous sense of inevitability for the two-state plan.

But if armies can't resist the power of an idea whose time has come, then diplomats cannot enforce a vision inherently out of focus. A fundamental flaw in the two-state plan is oscillation of Palestinian Arab politics between the thuggish corruption of Yasir Arafat's Palestinian Authority and the murderous bigotry of Sheik Ahmed Yassin's Islamic Resistance Move-

Eric L. Rozenman, "Anatomy of an Illusion: The Israeli-Palestinian Two-State Solution," *Midstream*, February/March 2003, pp. 13–18. Copyright © 2003 by The Theodor Herzl Foundation. Reproduced by permission.

ment (Hamas). A November 2002 public opinion poll showed that while 76 percent of West Bank and Gaza Strip residents supported a mutual cessation of hostilities between Arabs and Israelis, only eight percent supported a Palestinian school curriculum teaching that Israel was legitimate and that peace could be reached without Arab control of all the former British Mandate for Palestine (Israel, Jordan, the West Bank and Gaza Strip).

So President Bush's "vision of two states, Israel and Palestine, side by side and at peace" remains inapplicable. Worse, attempting to reach it via "the road map" drawn by the United States with its other quartet partners—Russia, the United Nations, and the European Union—would prove to be a highway to hell. Like the Oslo "peace process,"[1] attempting actually to follow the road map and force such a state into existence during the next three years (Bush's timeline) appears likely to provoke more, not less, violence.

Short of a U.S.-led trusteeship for the territories, proposed in December [2002] by former U.S. Ambassador to Israel Martin Indyk, echoing Allied occupation of post–World War II West Germany and Japan, a peaceful Palestinian Arab democracy in the West Bank and Gaza Strip seems improbable. Yet, an America that assures one ally, Turkey, that it will not permit an independent Kurdistan to arise from the ruins of a post-[Iraqi president Saddam Hussein] Iraq and that sent troops half-way around the world to root out Afghanistan's Taliban and their Al Qaeda guests[2], would endanger a second ally, Israel, with creation of an Arafatia or Hamastan.

What doomed the two-state approach

Elements do exist for a compromise Israeli-Palestinian settlement. To recognize them one should first clarify what doomed the "two-state" approach. As adopted implicitly by the administrations of Presidents George W.H. Bush and Bill Clinton, this "vision" supported the 1993–2000 Oslo process. President George W. Bush's explicit endorsement is meant to resurrect that process from the ruins to which Arafat and the Palestinian leadership consigned it. But Oslo, a response to the 1987–1992 intifada [or "uprising"], ended by encouraging the much greater violence of the Al Aqsa intifada that began in September 2000 and in its first 27 months resulted in 680 Israeli dead, mostly civilian, and 1,700 Palestinian dead, mostly combatants or violent demonstrators. Attempting to force the two-state solution now could likely transform the Palestinians' "war of independence and return" into a regional war.

The Al Aqsa intifada should have been no surprise. Endorsements of the two-state solution rewarded previous Palestinian violence and provided incentives for more. [In June of 2002], the president and his spokesmen were still promoting such a settlement in conjunction with visits of Egyptian President Hosni Mubarak and Saudi Arabian Foreign Minister Saud al-Faisal. That made sense, since American support for the quartet road map to a two-state solution is meant to bolster the brittle regimes in Cairo, Riyadh, and Amman. These unrepresentative governments fear

1. In 1993, negotiations between Israel and the Palestinians were conducted in Oslo, Norway.   2. The Taliban provided refuge for terrorist Osama bin Laden's organization al-Qaeda, the group responsible for the September 11, 2001, terrorist attacks on America.

popular discontent—including discontent inflamed by Israeli resistance to Palestinian aggression and a U.S.-Iraqi war. So even with suicide bombers back in action, the European Union insisted again [in 2002] that Israel concede Palestinian demands. This reminded Israel's enemies that violence pays. British Prime Minister Tony Blair's December [2002] call for a conference of Arab officials in London to advance the two-state plan acknowledged that Palestinian reform was not a necessary condition.

Palestinian Arab leadership rejected partition of western Palestine, unfailingly, from the 1920s to the present.

Granting the Palestinian Arabs the West Bank and Gaza Strip in exchange for peace with an Israel back behind the pre-1967 "green line" [the original limit of Israeli territory] possessed a certain logic. But logic was not reality. As Benny Morris, an Israeli historian sympathetic to the Arabs' sense of grievance, put it: "The logical solution is partition. Unfortunately, it's a solution that the Arabs have consistently rejected. If they continue to reject a two-state solution, one people will ultimately prevail. There will be one state here. Whoever is stronger will win."

Palestinian Arab leadership rejected partition of western Palestine, unfailingly, from the 1920s to the present. Those rejections included massacres of Jews in 1921 and 1929; the "revolt" from 1936 to 1939 . . . , the war against the U.N. Partition Plan in 1947 and 1948; terrorism against Israel from 1948 to 1967 (before Israel gained the West Bank, or Judea and Samaria, and the Gaza Strip); renewed terrorism after 1967 when a victorious Israel initially proposed to return most of the territories in exchange for peace; rejection of the 1979 autonomy provisions of the Egyptian-Israeli peace treaty; refusal to halt terrorism during the 1993–1998 Oslo process that otherwise would have yielded West Bank and Gaza self-rule after five years; and rejection of a state on 95 percent of the territories and eastern Jerusalem as well after the Camp David meeting in July 2000.

Attempts to impose peace between Jews and Palestinian Arabs by confirming the former in possession of "Israel proper" and the latter in a sovereign Gaza Strip and West Bank state consistently ignore widespread Arab rejection of Israel in any boundaries. . . .

Arab rejectionism continues

The Al Aqsa intifada [which began in 2000] reaffirmed that although Arafat and the Palestinian Authority grudgingly acknowledged Israel's existence, neither Palestinian nationalists nor Islamic fundamentalists accepted its legitimacy. Peace treaties with Egypt and Jordan notwithstanding, rejection of Jewish statehood is a commonplace throughout much of the Arab-Islamic world. If not, King Abdullah II of Jordan's statement to *The Times* of London in November 2001 that recognition by the Arab world of Israel's right to exist "will be necessary for the creation of a Palestinian state" would have been superfluous. That rejection, abetted by elites in Egypt and Jordan as well as Saudi Arabia to deflect internal unrest onto the Jewish state and the Jews, ultimately destabilizes those governments as well as chances for Israeli-Palestinian peace.

By word and deed Palestinian leadership, whether that of Arafat or Sheik Yassin, made clear it cannot or will not be a partner to a settlement according to the letter and spirit of [UN] Resolution 242. The measure, adopted after the 1967 war, calls for an end to states of belligerency among the parties to the combat (including Syria, Egypt, Jordan, Iraq, and Israel), the right of all states to secure and recognized borders, Israeli military withdrawal from territory (not from all the territory) taken in the fighting, and, among other things, a just solution to the refugee problem (Arab and Jewish refugees).

Resolution 338, adopted after the 1973 Yom Kippur War between Egypt, Syria, and Israel, calls on the parties to begin negotiations to implement Resolution 242. Unlike non-binding General Assembly resolutions, Security Council measures carry the weight of international law.

Given that demography and geography circumscribe diplomacy, a West Bank and Gaza Strip state—even if accepted by the Palestinians—could not satisfy Israel's minimal requirements. First, it could serve as a springboard to renewed Palestinian assault, as intifada II demonstrates. Second, even with full compliance regarding limitations on police and weaponry and requirements to eradicate the terrorist infrastructure, a two-state solution would not provide Israel with the minimally necessary, defensible borders in the event of another general Arab-Israeli war.

After the fighting in 1967, the U.S. Joint Chiefs of Staff advised President Lyndon Johnson that, absent peace, Israel would have to retain the western half of the Golan Heights, the western slopes of Samaria (the northern West Bank), much of Judea (the southern West Bank), the southwestern Gaza strip and most of the Sinai Peninsula (returned in phases under the 1979 Egyptian-Israeli peace treaty). After the '73 Yom Kippur War, a U.S. Army analysis by Col. Irving Kett revisited the problem and came to a similar conclusion.

As Yitzhak Rabin declared to the Knesset on June 3, 1974 during his first term as prime minister, "It is essential that the leaders of the neighboring countries realize that Israel is entitled to defensible borders. Israel will not return—even within the context of a peace treaty—to the June 4, 1967 lines. These lines are not defensible borders, and they constitute a temptation for aggression against us, as has been proven in the past." Rabin said the same thing 20 years later, a year after the handshake on the White House lawn, and Housing and Construction Minister Natan Sharansky more recently made the same point: the pre-'67 lines prohibit peace based on deterrence.

Conditions for Israel's security

Former Israeli chief of staff and foreign minister, Yigal Allon, proposed to meet Israeli security needs, to escape the demographic dangers inherent in ruling over large numbers of Arabs, and to open the way to a regional settlement (*Foreign Affairs*, October, 1976). Among other things, Allon recommended that, to retain minimum defensive depth, Israel (less than 10 miles wide at several points along its populous coastal strip before 1967) do the following:

- Annex the sparsely populated Jordan Valley, a deep, narrow, natural tank trap;
- Annex the small but strategic Etzion bloc (held by Jews before 1948) just south of Jersalem;
- Thicken the coastal strip north of Tel Aviv with a contiguous sliver of westernmost Samaria;
- Annex southwestern Gaza; and,
- Retain Jerusalem in enlarged city limits as Israel's united capital.

Allon envisioned that most of the territory, and nearly all of its Arab population, would be returned to Jordan in exchange for recognition, diplomatic relations, and peace. In 1986, Saul Cohen, a political geographer and president emeritus of Queens College of the City University of New York, in "The Geopolitics of Israel's Border Question," for Tel Aviv University's Jaffe Center for Strategic Studies, proposed an intricate, reduced update of Allon. It required annexation of 20 percent of the West Bank, 19 percent of the Gaza Strip, and long-term arrangements short of annexation in the lower Jordan Valley and connecting corridors through the West Bank (as well as half the Golan Heights). Rabin's 1992 campaign platform reaffirmed Allon's guidelines.

A two-state solution would not provide Israel with the minimally necessary, defensible borders in the event of another general Arab-Israeli war.

Since it came under Israeli control in 1967, the Arab population of the West Bank, Gaza Strip, and eastern Jerusalem has surged to more than three million. Israel, with a population of five million Jews and 1.3 million Arabs, cannot annex populated portions of the territories—even if necessary for military purposes—without endangering its status as a Jewish state. Neither can it build a wall unilaterally separating itself from the territories, as now being done in fits and starts, and assure its Jewish future by huddling inside that barrier. Certainly this is not possible while a militarized Palestine rockets it from the other side and Israel itself retains a radicalized Arab population of 21 percent (up from 16 percent in 1967 and growing faster than the Jewish majority, even after the immigration influx from the former Soviet Union).

As for Palestinian Arabs, much less than the entire West Bank and Gaza Strip (an area a little larger than Delaware, as Israel, pre-'67, approximates Massachusetts) would yield a stunted sovereignty. Lacking a hinterland, the Palestinian state would of necessity covet both Israel and Jordan, the former with its Arabs increasingly identifying as Palestinians, the latter with Palestinians comprising nearly three-fourths of its 4.5 million population.

Possible alternatives

What then is the alternative? Perhaps a real two-state solution in Mandatory Palestine, Allon-minus for the Jews, Oslo-minus for the Palestinians.

As minimal as Allon's ideas seemed to Israelis, they never came close to winning approval of even moderate Arabs. The latter's interpretation of Resolution 242—instigated by the Soviets in contradiction to its diplomatic history—was "all the land for any peace." But such a settlement would then and now have contradicted 242's insistence on borders both secure and recognized.

The key, as Allon noted, is "fair political compromise . . . likely to be painful in the short term to both sides." To both sides—Jews and Arabs, not three sides, Israelis, Palestinians, and Jordanians.

There is no room, geographically, demographically, economically, militarily, or otherwise for two sovereign, equal states.

Anyone who has stood in Ariel, the Israeli "settlement" (a modern town of 14,000 Jews) just before sunset and watched the Dead Sea fade into shadow below and to the east, and the lights flicker on along Tel Aviv's shoreline below and to the west, understands. There is no room, geographically, demographically, economically, militarily, or otherwise for two sovereign, equal states in the 40- to 45-mile wide, 180-mile long strip west of the Jordan River between Lebanon and the Negev Desert—and definitely not when the people of one state cheer their children's murder/suicides in the other.

But already there are, as there have been for more than half a century, two states—one Arab and one Jewish—in old Mandatory Palestine. This is not to say, as some on the Israeli right, including Prime Minister Sharon, used to, that "Jordan is Palestine" but rather to note that not only was Jordan Palestine, but so also Israel and the West Bank and Gaza Strip (and, initially, the Golan Heights). To be precise, Jordan comprises 77 percent of the old mandate, Israel inside the pre-'67 "green line" 17 percent, and the West Bank and Gaza the remaining six.

The Jewish state in Palestine requires borders more expansive than those of June 4, 1967. This is especially so since a demilitarized West Bank and Gaza Arab Palestine, isolated from Syria, Iraq, and Iran, as stipulated by proponents of the two-state solution, is a fiction, as noted above. Israel's own failures and international futility regarding [the terrorist group] Hezbollah in the ostensibly U.N.-patrolled south Lebanon "security zone," Arafat's illegally enlarged, illegally armed "police" and Palestinian militia, and the nearly two-and-a-half-year assault on Israeli cities and towns by gunmen, suicide bombers, mortar crews, and rocket launchers testify to that.

Meanwhile, the Arab population on the remaining West Bank and Gaza Strip will require territorial and economic depth on which meaningful sovereignty can be exercised. An arid, over-crowded entity the size of four smallish American counties cannot suffice.

Therefore, the remaining unallocated portion of Mandatory Palestine—the West Bank and Gaza Strip—must be divided between two states. Jordan and Israel, Arab Palestine and Jewish Palestine. The shape of this territorial compromise also is relatively clear. Before launching intifada II, the Palestinian Authority already controlled or shared control with Israel of 54 percent of the territory (which includes the vast majority of the Palestinian population). Prior to his Camp David II proposal, fears of which sundered his own government, [former Israeli prime minister Ehud] Barak insisted on a "red line" minimum of 10 percent of the disputed territories. Roughly splitting the difference, one arrives at an 80-20 percent compromise approximately along the lines of Professor Cohen's 1986 proposal.

This cannot be implemented, of course, so long as Arafat and Sheik Yassin represent the two poles of Palestinian Arab politics, so long as Palestinian Arabs in Lebanon, Syria, and Jordan believe they are "going home" to Israel. As in post-Taliban Afghanistan, or perhaps a post-Saddam Hussein Iraq, positive developments require the defeat—military and diplomatic—of rejectionist Palestinian nationalism and emboldened Islamic terrorism.

Conditions for resolution

Real nation building in the West Bank and Gaza Strip probably must await, as *The Wall Street Journal* editorialized in "Arabs and Democracy," April 3, 2002, the replacement of Saddam Hussein's dictatorial regime. "That means," the editorialist noted, "not merely toppling Saddam . . . but staying long enough to underwrite an election under United Nations auspices. The Iranian people, already restive under the mullahs, would then take heed and liberate themselves. Arab leaders throughout the Middle East would have to adapt to the same lesson, including the Palestinians. . . . The violence in Palestine doesn't need another mediator; it needs an outside shock that changes Arab assumptions about what is possible. It needs a pro-Western Iraq on the road to democracy."

A "three-state solution" to the problem of Palestine—for that is what an arrangement of Israel, Jordan and West Bank/Gaza Strip Palestine would amount to—resembles the tinder of post-[Yugoslavian leader Josef] Tito Croatia, Serbia, and Bosnia,[3] waiting for a match. A real two-state solution—one Arab, one Jewish—based on changed assumptions all around about what is sustainable, would contribute to regional stability, lessen the chances of regional war, and promote U.S. interests. President Bush's June 24 "vision" shocked the Palestinians, the Egyptians, the Jordanians, and the Saudis. It did the same to the Europeans and the Israeli left. The quartet's road map—to be followed regardless of Palestinian reform or geographic and demographic reality—dissipates that healthful shock and returns to a deadly cul-de-sac.

---

3. Croatia, Serbia, and Bosnia were all republics within Yugoslavia, which began to break apart in the early 1990s.

11

A Security Wall Is Necessary for Israel's Survival

Ofer Zur

Ofer Zur, formally an officer in the Israeli army, is currently a clinical psychologist living in California.

Bloodshed in the Middle East is concentrated in areas where the Israeli army is protecting small Jewish settlements in a vast Palestinian population. Any Palestinian gunman or suicide bomber can walk into these settlements and kill Israelis. As peace may be impossible because of the long-standing distrust between Israelis and Palestinians, a wall must be built to forcibly separate the Israeli and Palestinian populations in order to guarantee the safety of both peoples. This would allow for healing over time, which might lead to peace in the distant future, but would almost certainly lessen the violence that currently perpetuates the conflict.

I was born into a family that takes pride in having four generations of marchers for peace. For many years, my sister was among the Women in Black who stood silently in support of peace at all major crossroads in Israel every Friday afternoon. My mother not only fought for Israel's independence, but also advocated for Arab women's rights back in the 1940s. My father's complementary message was Zionism and the love of all nations

At eighteen years young, I was inducted into the Israeli Army, as are all young men and women in Israel. I got my paratrooper wings and served as an officer. Before the first intifada [or Palestinian uprising] during the late 1960s and early 1970s, I had already paid the moral and spiritual price of being part of an occupying force. I shot at a crowd of youths who were frighteningly and quickly closing in on me; I participated in the demolition of houses belonging to families of "terrorist suspects," I enforced erratic curfews on 80,000 people in a refugee camp; and I followed orders to round up "young adults" for random interrogation. All these took their toll on me, as they have also on the spirit of thousands of other Israeli soldiers who have served in the occupied territories over

Ofer Zur, "Time for a Wall," *Tikkun*, vol. 17, May 2002, pp. 20–22. Copyright © 2002 by The Institute for Labor and Mental Health. Reproduced by permission.

the last three decades. Above all, the Occupation has taken a toll on the collective soul of Israel and the hearts of Jews everywhere, whether they admit it or are even aware of it. . . .

> *It has certainly been true that the peace movement in Israel has lapsed into silence.*

There were brief periods of hope [for reconciliation] after [former Egyptian president Anwar Sadat's] visit to Jerusalem in 1977 and the Oslo Agreement of 1993,[1] but that hope died with [former Israeli Prime Minister Yitzhak] Rabin in 1995. A briefer period of hope in 1999–2000 was kindled by [former Israeli prime minister] Ehud Barak, who seemed to offer the most far-reaching peace proposals ever. [Palestinian leader Yasir] Arafat's refusal to accept Barak's proposals and the beginning of the current Palestinian uprising, the second intifada, changed the political picture, in my opinion, permanently. It has certainly been true that the peace movement in Israel has lapsed into silence. The rejection of Barak's offer and the endless killings and suicide bombings have left the movement feeling bitter towards Arafat and simultaneously drawn toward an uncomfortable consensus with the Right, a consensus that the Palestinian people are not to be trusted or considered a serious partner for peace.

Seven thousand miles away from Israel, looking at the situation from the idyllic comfort and beauty of the wine country in Northern California, it is clear to me why the Palestinians did not accept Barak's proposals, why they demanded nothing less than full autonomy over the entire West Bank and the Gaza Strip with East Jerusalem as their capital. From my eminence in Northern California, it did not make sense that 200,000 settlers, residing in dozens of settlements all over the West Bank in the midst of more than two million Palestinians were allowed to keep escalating the conflict, bloodshed, and immense suffering on all sides in their relentless pursuit of the Greater Israel dream (Of course the mirror image of this is [the Islamic militant group] Hamas' image of a "Greater Palestine" where the Jews are finally driven into the sea).

The hard reality

What has also become apparent, although missing from most of the CNN or *New York Times* news reports on Middle East, is the simple but essential fact that most of the daily violence and casualties in the region occur in specific areas and stem from one source. The bloodshed comes from the fact that the Israeli army is heavily present all over the West Bank and Gaza Strip in order to defend dozens and dozens of primarily small settlements strategically located in the midst of the Palestinian population. It is quite normal for a few thousand soldiers to be engaged in the defense of a couple dozen families. The army protects the settlers' bulletproof school buses, their main crossroads, the strategic positions in the area, the

1. The Oslo Agreement set the conditions for Israeli-Palestinian peace. The agreement was named after the talks held in Oslo, Norway.

settlers' "right" to freely drive the West Bank roads and, of course, the settlements themselves. While most of the news reports focus on suicide bombers in Jerusalem or Tel Aviv, the presence of the settlers and the army all over the occupied territories and especially at the road-blocked main junctions, where humiliating and demeaning searches take place, fuel the daily violence and death toll in the region. For the Palestinians, the army/settlers combination is the most powerful symbol of the harsh reality of the Occupation.

I remember guarding a tiny settlement occupied mostly by a handful of New Yorkers in the midst of a dense Palestinian population in the West Bank. I vividly recall the dramatic contrast between the lush green lawns and refreshing swimming pool of the settlement and the yellow, dying crops and rationed water of the neighboring Palestinian villages. The contrast was overwhelming.

Given the amount of bloodshed in recent days and months and years, peace is not even a remote option at this point.

The reality of the region these days is destruction, injury, and death, and it is not about to change very soon. The [2002] withdrawal of the Israeli army from Southern Lebanon brought a revelation to the Palestinians. They realized that Israel could not stomach the human cost of occupation indefinitely. Palestinians are also aware that Israel is gradually losing its moral ground and sympathy not only in the eyes of the world, but also in the eyes of the many Jews who have supported Israel unconditionally for so long. Accordingly, the Palestinians are willing to continue sacrificing their lives and the lives of their children for the cause of liberating Palestine. At the same time, the settlers are just as willing to sacrifice themselves and their children for their cause. . . .

The present situation, in which any suicide bomber or gunman can simply walk across from the West Bank into Israel, is becoming increasingly intolerable for Israelis. The eye-for-an-eye and bomb-for-a-bomb exchanges of the last few months have resulted in hundreds of dead and wounded on both sides. Given the amount of bloodshed in recent days and months and years, peace is not even a remote option at this point in time. Unlike the memory of many Americans, which at best is as long as the next quarterly corporate report, Middle Eastern memory goes back thousands of years. Accordingly, any talk of peace in the region is ludicrous when one realizes the extent of death, injury, and, above all, betrayal, which both sides have sustained in the last decade.

The wall is necessary

Peace now is impossible. This leaves Israel with only one viable option: the unilateral, forced separation of the territories, to be achieved by building a wall and/or creating a buffer zone to physically separate Israel from Palestine.

Such a unilateral division would not require negotiation, agreement, pre-, or post-conditions. . . . It would not require endorsement by any Arab country. It is based neither on trust nor on love and it will not bring immediate peace or tolerance or love. What this pragmatic, concrete separation will do is serve to reduce the violence between the Palestinians and Israelis significantly. At the very least, it will make it harder for any Palestinian youth with explosives strapped to his (and most recently her) body, to cross into Israeli territory. A wall may never have wide international recognition, but it will allow the Israelis and the Palestinians to spend another forty (or better—one hundred) years in the desert, letting the sharp pain of loss dull a bit, and allowing a new generation to grow up without experiencing the injuries, hatred, and fear of their neighbor. Only then will peace be a possibility. The wall will provide an obstacle to violence and will buy time so that wounds can gradually heal. "Gradually," in the Middle East, may mean a few or many generations.

A wall is not a new idea, nor will it easily be accepted by the Right or the Left in Israel. The Right is appropriately concerned that such a wall would mean the end of their dream of a Greater Israel, and the diminution of their hopes to expel the Palestinians. Above all, this proposal will highlight the Right's concern about the future of the settlements which will come under Palestinian rule. For the remaining members of the Left, this proposal will revive bitter memories of the wall that divided Jerusalem before the Six Day War and, of course, grim memories of the Berlin Wall and the DMZ [or demilitarized zone] between North and South Korea.

The wall will provide an obstacle to violence and will buy time so that wounds can gradually heal.

Yet a wall must be built. To be successful, this wall must be built on the Green line, along the pre-1967 borders of Israel, with only the slightest modifications—for example, the inclusion of sections of Jerusalem where the Jews constituted a majority of the population as of the year 2000 . . . (so as to exclude the possibility that right-wingers will begin to expand their settlements in East Jerusalem [in the future]). The wall will not be successful if it is built as part of an occupational plan to incorporate and annex big parts of the West Bank into Israel (along the lines of the "buffer zones" contemplated by [Israeli prime minister] Ariel Sharon), because battle and bloodshed will continue, despite a wall, until Israel agrees to a Palestinian State that is close enough in size and shape to the original West Bank territories which were conquered in 1967.

Benefits of a wall

Consider the following points in favor of such a forced separation:

1. It can be completed unilaterally by Israel.
2. It does not require lengthy negotiation and the sort of endless preconditions that have rendered almost all negotiations hopeless.
3. Building such a wall need not be based on trust or love of the Palestinians.
4. The wall will consist of a real wall and/or fences, and neutral zones

where security will be augmented by electronic technology, explosives, satellites and other sophisticated devices. This will enhance the overall security of Israel's borders.

5. Separation will make it very hard for any suicide bomber to simply cross the border into Tel Aviv or Jerusalem and blow themselves up.

6. Israel will retain control over entries along the Jordan River from Jordan to Palestine for the sole purpose of preventing heavy arms from being smuggled into the Palestinian State.

7. The wall will have a few major crossing points where Palestinian laborers and Palestinian goods, under intense Israeli scrutiny, can cross into Israel. These laborers are much needed by both Israel's and Palestine's economies.

8. The Gaza Strip, which will also be surrounded by a wall (in fact, some fenced buffer zones already exist), will be connected to the West Bank via a direct, high security, fenced, non-stop suspended highway. The technology for a fast rail for both passengers and goods is also readily available. This, for the first time, will make possible a cohesive Palestinian State.

9. The separation will enable the Palestinians to focus on their state's affairs. These internal affairs are likely to be complex, numerous, and, regretfully, highly volatile.

10. Israeli armed forces will be categorically excluded from the Palestinian side of the wall. If hostility is initiated from the Palestinian side, Israel will respond the same way it would respond if Egypt, Jordan, Syria, or Iraq had initiated it. As we all know, Israel, having one of the most powerful and sophisticated armies in the world, is thoroughly capable of protecting itself by military and other means.

11. The settlers presently located in the occupied territories will have to choose to move into Israel or risk staying under Palestinian control.

12. In the short run, such a separation will put an end to the role of Israelis as an occupying force and will enable Israel's citizens, its soldiers, and Jews around the world to begin to heal from the wounds of the Occupation.

13. Such a unilateral separation will hopefully lead to a less volatile atmosphere in the region. Hopefully, this will translate into a stable, albeit cautious, coexistence and, ultimately, into real peace.

Day after one more tragic day, I have watched the carnage—angry, sad, and impotent, paralyzed by the growing violence. The Right seems to feed the flames; the Left seems hopelessly naive and silenced; the great and small powers of the world are repetitive and simplistic, failing to grasp the depth of the differences and complexities of this conflict. Even the most reasonable say "There is no solution." Israel and Palestine are trapped on a deadly carousel, repeating horror after horror, around and around, faster and faster. Israel must act. Knowing that I am abandoning the dream of my parents, the dream of peace in our lifetimes, I cannot avoid the obvious conclusion. First, the carousel must be stopped; Israel must build a wall and force a physical separation. Then, time may do its slow work. Indeed, mine is not a true solution, only a necessary circumvention. But we must try. There is no longer any other acceptable or sane alternative.

12

Israel's Security Wall Will Harm the Palestinians

Mariam Shahin

Mariam Shahin is a freelance journalist who works in the Middle East. Her articles have appeared in the London Independent, *the* Guardian, *and the* Christian Science Monitor.

The Israeli security wall being built between Jewish settlements and the Palestinian population in disputed Palestinian territories is a flawed and dangerous solution to the Israeli-Palestinian conflict. It might provide a small measure of protection for Israeli settlers in the West Bank but is doing so by making the Palestinians prisoners. Walls have been erected before during the history of the Israeli-Palestinian conflict and have not worked to bring peace. The only logical reason for erecting the wall is to allow further Israeli annexation of Palestinian territory. If the international community fails to stop the wall's construction, there will be insufficient land remaining for an independent Palestinian state.

[S oon] the concrete foundations of a wall, eight metres high and more than 250 miles long, which will effectively imprison the Palestinians of the West Bank, will be in place. Preparations for construction of the wall began [in June 2002]. The first section will stretch for 72 miles from Salem village, west of Jenin, forming a loop around the city of Qalqilya, the closest West Bank town to the Mediterranean and only eight miles from Tel Aviv. Israel has made preparations by encircling Qalqilya with a 10-foot fence and barbed wire confiscating over 55% of the surrounding arable land. There is only one way out—with Israeli permission—and the Israelis rarely grant permits to leave. The Israeli government calls the wall "the separation fence" and says it will contain suicide bombers. The Palestinians say the wall is not protecting Israeli citizens but instead protecting Israel's occupation, its illegal colonies and its ongoing colonisation of Palestinian land.

Thanks to an electrically wired concrete fence, twice as long and three times as high as the Berlin Wall, the Palestinian-Israeli dance of death will

Mariam Shahin, "The Wall, This New Obscenity," *The Middle East*, January 2002, pp. 6–9. Copyright © 2002 by IC Publications Ltd. Reproduced by permission.

be incubated until a more viable solution can be found, according to Israeli liberals.

To be constructed east of Israel's 1967 border inside the Occupied Palestinian Territory, the 250 mile "security" wall will de facto annex yet more Palestinian land. This is to some extent consistent with Israeli government policies, both Likud and Labor [Israel's conservative and liberal political parties, respectively], which have repeatedly said Israel will not return to the pre-1967 border, thus further annexation is nothing but more of the same. Not only is Israel building a wall, it has also begun erecting militarily enforced electrified fences around Palestinian controlled "Area A" (consisting of approximately 17.2% of the West Bank). The wall, the fences and the new restrictions of movement imposed on Arabs mean Palestinians will effectively be caged into 13 separate Israeli-created ghettos.

This wall is nothing new

The concept of a wall to keep people in or out is an age-old practice among totalitarian governments and regimes. In the Middle Ages, undesirable groups were confined to ghettos in European cities, making their presence in areas outside their specified quarters illegal and punishable by law. Outlaws were similarly caged in by barbed wire walls and fences as were native peoples of lands conquered by Europeans in the "colonies", particularly the United States and Australia.

And this will not be the first wall in the history of the Israeli-Palestinian conflict. The wall or fence dividing the Arab ruled part of Palestine from Jewish controlled Palestine, which subsequently became Israel, was made famous by the Mandelbaum Gate, at which mostly Arab families would pass on letters and oral messages to each other through barbed wire. The wall and gate became obsolete in 1967 when Israel occupied all of British Mandate Palestine. Then in 1987–1993, a "security" wall was built around the Gaza Strip, with a sealed electrical fence. This fence allowed Israel to maintain its 16 colonial settlements in the Gaza Strip and control Palestinian movement. Despite the Oslo Accords[1] Israel has not dismantled a single Gaza settlement and continues to control about 60% of Gaza, keeping the 1.2 [million] Palestinian residents under virtual siege.

This will not be the first wall in the history of the Israeli-Palestinian conflict.

Building layers of walls inside the West Bank means the Palestinians living there will soon share the fate of their co-nationals in the Gaza Strip. As well as their freedom, they will also lose homes, arable land and water resources. At least some of the $14 [billion] in aid and soft loans Israel has requested from the US government will go towards construction of the wall, which, it is estimated, will cost around $1.7 [million] a mile to build. The fortifications in the northern West Bank consist of a fortified eight

1. The Oslo Accords were conditions set for Israeli-Palestinian peace in the early 1990s.

metre-high cement structure, with watchtowers situated every 300 metres, flanked by a two metre-deep trench, barbed wire and a security road.

In East Jerusalem the wall separates Arab and Israeli areas with electric wire fencing and a security road, at certain points also combined with trenches, cement walls and motion detectors.

All Palestinian property (including homes, farms, fields and greenhouses) within 35 metres of the wall will be destroyed by Israeli forces.

Encouraged by the lack of international condemnation or any action to prevent these illegal activities, the Israeli government is forging ahead with its plan, also building smaller walls inside the West Bank so that nearly every refugee camp, village and town is enclosed by a fence or a wall, surrounded by barbed wire, with machine gun carrying Israeli soldiers in strategically placed look out towers above. When the wall from the northern West Bank to Jerusalem is completed, Israel will have annexed another 7% of the West Bank, 39 illegal Israeli colonial settlements (with 270,000 settlers), and 290,000 Palestinians. About one third of these Palestinians do not currently have Israeli residency and are not likely to get it, which means they must move, be deported, or go to jail for squatting, illegal presence or any other reason the Israeli government might concoct. If the building of the wall continues south to Hebron, Israel will then have annexed a further 3% of the West Bank.

The future of Palestine

There seems to be a consensus among the international community, which supports a re-starting of final status negotiations on Palestine within the next three to five years. This ignores however, the fact that very little will be left to negotiate over, and certainly not enough for an independent viable Palestinian state. Many on the Israeli left celebrated the decision to build the wall—a move long opposed by the right wing and settlers—as a final recognition by Israel that a two-state solution is inevitable. But celebration hardly seems in order when one considers what kind of state the wall will produce for the Arabs. It will certainly place even greater restrictions on space. At some points the structure reaches as far as three miles into Palestinian territory east of the Green Line, the armistice line of the 1948 war, beyond which UN resolutions require Israel to withdraw.

One of the first communities to be affected is the city of Qalqilya, which includes 32 villages, 72,000 Palestinians and 19 illegal Israeli colonies with an estimated illegal Israeli settler population of 50,700. With 40,000–45,000 Palestinian residents living on approximately 900 acres, Qalqilya has an additional 1,600 acres of agricultural land that surrounds the city. More importantly it sits on top of one of the three major aquifer basins in the Occupied West Bank. This aquifer basin produces approximately half of the Occupied West Bank's water resources. However, the Qalqilya section of the wall is built in such a way as to give Israel almost total control of the most productive zones of the aquifer basin.

"Qalqilya used to export fruit and vegetables as far as the Gulf," explained the mayor, Marouf Zahran, as he stood on the edge of fields now off limits to Palestinian farmers. "Now we are wondering how we can have enough food to feed our own people."

As a special incentive for Palestinians to stay in Qalqilya, all Palestinian property (including homes, farms, fields and greenhouses) within 35 metres of the wall will be destroyed by Israeli forces. Already bulldozers have cut a swathe through olive groves and orchards and the worst is yet to come; though nobody knows for sure where the Israeli axe will fall next. Neither schools nor hospitals are exempt—if they stand in the proposed path of the wall—they will be demolished.

So far four entrances to the city have already been militarily blocked and the remaining entrance has been turned into a military fortified gateway. . . .

Attacks, or alleged attacks by [the terrorist group] Al Qaeda, including the Paradise Mombasa Hotel massacre [in November 2002], which claimed the lives of 13, including mainly local African entertainers, have struck . . . fear into the heart of the international community. Washington, New York, Tel Aviv and London have declared themselves on red alert.

From Israel and the Occupied Territories the tales of carnage continue relentlessly: Israeli civilians, Arab youths, a 95 year old Palestinian great-grandmother returning from a trip to buy sweets for the local children, all killed in a hail of shrapnel or bullets. In the face of such horror [it] is not difficult to imagine how the focus of the international community might not be concentrated on the construction of a wall. However, if no objection is made, if no stand is taken, at this stage, by governments, human rights organisations, international agencies or sympathetic politicians, within months the Palestinians of the West Bank will have been corralled, like animals, behind that eight metre high, 250 mile long, electrically wired concrete wall, reinforced by razor wire. And by then long experience tells us, it will be too late.

Organizations to Contact

The editors have compiled the following list of organizations concerned with the issues debated in this book. The descriptions are derived from materials provided by the organizations. All have publications or information available for interested readers. The list was compiled on the date of publication of the present volume; names, addresses, phone and fax numbers, and e-mail addresses may change. Be aware that many organizations take several weeks or longer to respond to inquiries, so allow as much time as possible.

The American Israel Public Affairs Committee (AIPAC)
440 First St. NW, Suite 600, Washington, DC 20001
(202) 639-5200 • fax: (202) 347-4918
e-mail: update@aipac.org • website: www.aipac.org

The American Israel Public Affairs Committee is the only registered lobby that works with Congress and the White House administration to strengthen the U.S.-Israeli relationship. AIPAC activists help pass more than one hundred pro-Israel legislative initiatives a year. From procuring nearly $3 billion in aid critical to Israel's security, to funding joint U.S.-Israeli efforts to build a defense against unconventional weapons, AIPAC members are involved in the most crucial issues facing Israel. AIPAC produces the *Near East Report*, a biweekly newsletter on American Middle East policy.

American Task Force on Palestine (ATFP)
815 Connecticut Ave. NW, Suite 1200, Washington, DC 20006
(202) 887-0177 • fax: (202) 887-1920
e-mail: atfp@atfp.net • website: www.americantaskforce.org

ATFP is an organization dedicated to bringing about lasting peace and stability in the Middle East by establishing the state of Palestine alongside Israel. ATFP plans to fulfill this mission of peace by coordinating the efforts of Americans of Palestinian heritage working with others in civic, educational, cultural, legal, economic, and political endeavors. The task force produces the *Daily Mideast News Roundup*, which is read each day by thousands of decision makers, academics, journalists, activists, and others around the world and has proven invaluable in presenting the Mideast conflict from multiple perspectives.

Human Rights Watch
350 Fifth Ave., 34th Floor, New York, NY 10118-3299
(212) 290-4700 • fax: (212) 736-1300
e-mail: hrwnyc@hrw.org • website: www.hrw.org

Human Rights Watch is dedicated to protecting the human rights of people around the world. It is an independent, nongovernmental organization, supported by contributions from private individuals and foundations worldwide, and the largest human rights organization based in the United States. Human Rights Watch conducts regular, systematic investigations of human rights abuses in more than seventy countries around the world, including Israel and

Palestine. The organization's reports describe human rights violations, detail the causes, and recommend how to end the abuses.

The Institute for Palestine Studies
3501 M St. NW, Washington, DC 20007
(202) 342-3990 • fax: (202) 342-3927
e-mail: ipsdc@palestine-studies.org • website: www.palestine-studies.org

The Institute for Palestine Studies is an independent, nonprofit, Arab research organization, not affiliated with any political organization or government. The institute is devoted to a better understanding of the question of Palestine. The Washington office serves as a publication and distribution coordinating center for the English publications of the institute. The *Journal of Palestine Studies*, one of the most important publications of the institute, is the only English-language quarterly devoted exclusively to the study of Palestinian affairs and the Arab-Israeli conflict.

The Islamic Association for Palestine (IAP)
Islamic Association for Palestine in North America
10661 South Roberts Rd., Suite 202, Palos Hills, IL 60465
(708) 974-3380 • fax: (708) 974-3389
e-mail: iapinfo@iap.org • website: www.iap.org

The Islamic Association for Palestine is a not-for-profit, educational organization dedicated to advancing a just, comprehensive, and eternal solution to the cause of Palestine and sufferings of the Palestinians. The IAP publishes the Arabic *Al-Zaytuna* biweekly newspaper and other special publications. It conducts studies of importance and makes the information available to the public.

Israel Ministry of Foreign Affairs
9 Yitzhak Rabin Blvd., Kiryat Ben-Gurion, Jerusalem 91035
972-2-530-3111 • fax: 972-2-530-3367
e-mail: feedback@mfa.gov.il • website: www.mfa.gov.il

The foreign ministry formulates, implements, and presents the foreign policy of the government of Israel. It represents the state vis-à-vis foreign governments and international organizations, explains the state's positions and problems throughout the world, endeavors to promote its economic, cultural, and scientific relations, and fosters cooperation with developing countries. The ministry's site links to several documents produced by the Israeli government, including official press releases and statements made by the prime minister.

The Jerusalem Fund: Palestine Center
2425-35 Virginia Ave. NW, Washington, DC 20037
(202) 338-1958 or (202) 338-1290 • fax: (202) 333-7742
e-mail: info@palestinecenter.org • website: www.palestinecenter.org

Established in 1991, the Palestine Center is the educational program of The Jerusalem Fund, a Washington-based, nonprofit, humanitarian organization. The center is dedicated to the study and analysis of the relationship between the United States and the Middle East, with particular emphasis on Palestine and the Arab-Israeli conflict. The center seeks to bring into focus the implications of specific U.S policies with regard to Palestine and the broader region. The center produces information and policy briefs, as well as special reports written by leading international experts. *The Conflict in the Middle East: The Breakdown of Peace* is the third edition of the center's annual compendium of reports, featuring briefs and articles published by the center between July 2001 and June 2002.

The Jewish Agency for Israel (JAFI)
633 Third Ave., 21st Floor, New York, NY 10017
(212) 339-6001 • fax: (212) 318-6155
e-mail: menachemr@jazo.org.il • website: www.jafi.org.il

As the world's major Jewish partnership organization, the Jewish Agency for Israel strives to strengthen the connection between Jews everywhere. The Jewish Agency sees its role as the emissary of global Jewry, forging close partnerships and facilitating opportunities for direct encounters between Israelis and Jews all over the world. Jewish Agency activities are brought to the attention of the media on an ongoing basis, through press releases, reports, photos, and timely and relevant highlighted activities—its website features these press releases. The JAFI also produces an electronic newsletter that highlights the latest articles in the *JAFI Magnet*, the organization's online news source.

The Palestinian Initiative for the Promotion of Global Dialogue and Democracy
PO Box 38588, Jerusalem 97800
972-2-585-1842 • fax: 972-2-583-5184
e-mail: info@miftah.org • website: www.miftah.org

The Palestinian Initiative, known as MIFTAH, an acronym derived from the organization's Arabic name, is a nongovernmental, nonpartisan, Jerusalem-based institution dedicated to fostering democracy and good governance within Palestinian society in a manner that promotes public accountability and transparency while maintaining the free flow of information and ideas. The organization produces *MIFTAH's Perspectives*, MIFTAH's main position paper, which is issued in the form of an essay on a continuous basis. It reflects MIFTAH's perspective on political developments related to the Israeli-Palestinian conflict.

Palestinian Liberation Organization: Negotiations Affairs Department (NAD)
Ministry of Information, Ramallah PO Box 224
972-2-295-4042 • fax: 972-2-295-4043
e-mail: minfo@minfo.gov.ps or postmaster@minfo.gov.ps
website: www.minfo.gov.ps

The Negotiations Affairs Department is an institution of the PLO that was established in 1994 in Gaza in order to follow up on the implementation of the Interim Agreement signed between Israel and the PLO. Since its establishment, the NAD has been headed by Mahmoud Abbas (Abu Mazen), secretary of the PLO Executive Committee. The NAD office in Gaza includes various units dealing primarily with Israeli affairs, Israeli violations of signed agreements, Israeli settlement activities, and refugees. The site links to statements and reports issued by the Palestinian government.

The United Nations
GA-57, New York, NY 10017
(212) 963-4475 • fax: (212) 963-0071
e-mail: inquiries@un.org
website: www.un.org/english or www.un.org/geninfo/faq

The United Nations was established on October 24, 1945, by fifty-one countries committed to preserving peace through international cooperation and collective security. Today, nearly every nation in the world belongs to the UN. The United Nations is not a world government and it does not make laws. It does, however, provide the means to help resolve international conflicts and formulate policies on matters affecting all of us. At the UN, all the member states—large and small, rich and poor, with differing political views and social systems—have a voice and a vote in this process. The UN produces many online and print publications, including the *United Nations Chronicle*, an easy-to-read, quarterly report on the work of the United Nations and its agencies.

U.S. Department of State
Bureau of Near Eastern Affairs Office of Public Affairs
Room 6242, 2201 C St. NW, Washington, DC 20520
(202) 647-5150 • fax: (202) 736-4462
website: www.state.gov/p/nea

The Bureau of Near Eastern Affairs, headed by Assistant Secretary William Joseph Burns, deals with U.S. foreign policy and U.S. diplomatic relations with these countries and geographic entities: Algeria, Bahrain, Egypt, Iran, Iraq, Israel, Jordan, Kuwait, Lebanon, Libya, Morocco, Oman, Qatar, Saudi Arabia, Syria, Tunisia, United Arab Emirates, and Yemen. The Department of State produces *Background Notes*, which are factual publications that contain information on all the countries of the world with which the United States has relations. These publications include facts on the country's land, people, history, government, political conditions, economy, and its relations with other countries and the United States.

The Zionist Organization of America (ZOA)
4 East 34th St., New York, NY 10016
(212) 481-1500 • fax: (212) 481-1515
e-mail: info@zoa.org • website: www.zoa.org

The Zionist Organization of America is the oldest, and one of the largest, pro-Israel organizations in the United States. Founded in 1897 to support the reestablishment of a Jewish state in the ancient land of Israel, its presidents have included such illustrious Jewish leaders as Supreme Court justice Louis D. Brandeis and Rabbi Abba Hillel Silver. The ZOA was instrumental in mobilizing the support of the U.S. government, Congress, and the American public for the creation of Israel in 1948. The organization publishes special reports, press releases, and articles on issues affecting Israel, most of which are available at the ZOA website.

Bibliography

Books

Mahmoud Abbas	*Through Secret Channels.* Reading, UK: Garnet, 1995.
Amnesty International	*Israel and the Occupied Territories: Excessive Use of Lethal Force.* London: International Secretariat, 2000.
Naseer Hasan Aruri	*Palestinian Refugees: The Right of Return.* Sterling, VA: Pluto Press, 2001.
Ian J. Bickerton and Carla L. Klausner	*A Concise History of the Arab-Israeli Conflict.* Upper Saddle River, NJ: Prentice-Hall, 2002.
Ian Black and Benny Morris	*Israel's Secret Wars: A History of Israel's Intelligence Services.* New York: Grove Weidenfeld, 1991.
Dan Cohn-Sherbok and Dawoud el-Alami	*The Palestine-Israeli Conflict: A Beginner's Guide.* Oxford, UK: Oneworld, 2001.
Alan Dershowitz	*The Case for Israel.* Hoboken, NJ: John Wiley, 2003.
Trevor Dupuy and Paul Martell	*Flawed Victory: The Arab-Israeli Conflict and the 1982 War in Lebanon.* Fairfax, VA: Hero Books, 1986.
Simha Flapan	*Zionism and the Palestinians.* London: Croom Helm, 1979.
Asad Ganim	*The Palestinian-Arab Minority in Israel, 1948–2000: A Political Study.* Albany: State University of New York Press, 2001.
Deborah J. Gerner, ed.	*Understanding the Contemporary Middle East.* Boulder, CO: Lynne Rienner, 2000.
Michael Goodspeed	*When Reason Fails: Portraits of Armies at War: America, Britain, Israel, and the Future.* Westport, CT: Praeger, 2002.
Meir Hatina	*Islam and Salvation in Palestine: The Islamic Jihad Movement.* Tel Aviv, Israel: The Moshe Dayan Center for Middle Eastern and African Studies, Tel Aviv University, 2001.
Theodor Herzl	*The Complete Diaries of Theodor Herzl.* New York: Herzl Press and T. Yoseloff, 1960.
Human Rights Watch	*Israel, the Occupied West Bank and Gaza Strip, and the Palestinian Authority Territories: Jenin: IDF Military Operations.* New York: Human Rights Watch, May 2002.
Effraim Karsh	*Israel: The First Hunderd Years.* Portland, OR: Frank Case, 2000.

Baruch Kimmerling and Joel Migdal	*Palestinians: The Making of a People.* Cambridge, MA: Harvard University Press, 1994.
Yaakov Kop and Robert E. Litan	*Sticking Together: The Israeli Experiment in Pluralism.* Washington, DC: Brookings Institution Press, 2002.
Shaul Mishal and Avraham Sela	*The Palestinian Hamas: Vision, Violence, and Coexistence.* New York: Columbia University Press, 2000.
Thomas G. Mitchell	*Native vs. Settler: Ethnic Conflict in Israel/Palestine, Northern Ireland, and South Africa.* Westport, CT: Greenwood Press, 2000.
Benny Morris	*Righteous Victims: A History of the Zionist Arab Conflict, 1881–2001.* New York: Vintage Books, 2001.
Farah Naaz	*The Road to Peace: The Israeli-Palestinian Conflict.* New Delhi, India: Institute for Defence Studies and Analyses, 2000.
Ilan Pappe	*The Making of the Arab-Israeli Conflict, 1947–1951.* London: I.B. Tauris, 1992.
Alisa Rubin Peled	*Debating Islam in the Jewish State: The Development of Policy Toward Islamic Institutions in Israel.* Albany: State University of New York Press, 2001.
Randall Price	*Unholy War: America, Israel and Radical Islam.* Eugene, OR: Harvest House, 2001.
Eugene L. Rogan	*The War for Palestine: Rewriting the History of 1948.* Cambridge, UK: Cambridge University Press, 2001.
Alwyn R. Rouyer	*Turning Water into Politics: The Water Issue in the Palestinian-Israeli Conflict.* New York: St. Martin's Press, 2000.
Amnon Rubinstein	*From Herzl to Rabin: The Changing Image of Zionism.* New York: Holmes & Meier, 2000.
Yezid Sayigh	*Armed Struggle and the Search for State: The Palestinian National Movement, 1949–1993.* Oxford, UK: Oxford University Press, 1997.
David Kenneth Schenker	*Palestinian Democracy and Governance: An Appraisal of the Legislative Council.* Washington, DC: Washington Institute for Near East Policy, 2000.
Avi Shlaim	*The Iron Wall: Israel and the Arab World.* New York: W.W. Norton, 2000.
Yisrael Tal	*National Security: The Israeli Experience.* Westport, CT: Praeger, 2000.
Mark Tessler	*A History of the Israeli-Palestinian Conflict.* Bloomington: Indiana University Press, 1994.
Bernard Wasserstein	*Divided Jerusalem: The Struggle for the Holy City.* New Haven, CT: Yale University Press, 2001.
Geoffrey R. Watson	*The Oslo Accords: International Law and the Israeli-Palestinian Peace Agreements.* Oxford, UK: Oxford University Press, 2000.

Periodicals

American Jewish Committee — "An Independent Palestinian State," *Commentary*, October 2003.

Jerold S. Auerbach — "Israel's Shadow Line," *Midstream*, April 2003.

Eugene Bird — "Traction . . . and Closed Negotiations," *Washington Report on Middle East Affairs*, July 2001.

Marwan Bishara — "Terrorism: The Way It Works," *World Press Review*, April 2002.

Ed Blanche — "Israel Faces War of Attrition as Intifada Reaches Critical Mass," *Jane's Intelligence Review*, April 2002.

Nicholas Blanford — "Hizbullah Prepares to Open Up Front Along the Israeli Border," *Jane's Intelligence Review*, April 2002.

Allan C. Brownfeld — "The Growing Danger of Transforming the Palestinian-Israeli Conflict into a Jewish-Muslim Religious War," *Washington Report on Middle East Affairs*, April 2001.

David B. Burrell — "Warring Stories," *Commonweal*, April 20, 2001.

Adel Darwish — "Get Out!" *Middle East*, May 2002.

David Eshel — "The Al-Aqsa Intifada: Tactics and Strategies (Israeli and Palestinian)," *Jane's Intelligence Review*, May 2001.

Thomas L. Friedman — "A Foul Wind," *New York Times*, March 10, 2002.

Shlomo Gazit and Edward Abington — "Upheaval in the Levant—the Palestinian-Israeli Conflict," *Middle East Policy*, 2001.

Wallace Greene — "Gracious Dialogue," *Midstream*, February/March 2003.

Lev Grinberg — "The Arrogance of Occupation," *Middle East Policy*, March 2002.

D.D. Guttenplan — "Parallax and Palestine: Divergence in British and American Views on the Middle East," *Nation*, March 11, 2002.

Joshua Hammer — "Lock Step," *New Republic*, December 31, 2001.

Mark Helprin — "What Israel Must Now Do to Survive," *Commentary*, November 2001.

Samah Jabr — "The Occupation Is Killing Us All: Silence and Security," *New Internationalist*, August 2002.

Rashid Khalidi — "The Centrality of Jerusalem to an End of Conflict Agreement," *Journal of Palestine Studies*, Spring 2001.

Louis Kriesberg — "Mediation and the Transformation of the Israeli-Palestinian Conflict," *Journal of Peace Research*, 2001.

Yehuda Lukacs — "America's Role—as the Israeli-Palestinian War of Attrition Enters Its Second Year, an Intense Debate Is Taking Place over the Content, Scope, and Future Direction of America's Policy in the Middle East," *World & I*, November 2001.

David Makovsky	"Middle East Peace Through Partition," *Foreign Affairs*, March/April 2001.
Camille Mansour	"The Impact of 11 September on the Israeli-Palestinian Conflict," *Journal of Palestine Studies*, 2002.
Elaine Pasquini	"Teach-In at College of Marin Examines Media Bias in Reporting Palestinian-Israeli Conflict," *Washington Report on Middle East Affairs*, May/June 2001.
Martin Peretz	"Enemies, a Love Story: G.W. Bush's Surprising Support for Israel," *New Republic*, April 9–16, 2001.
Ron Pundak	"From Oslo to Taba: What Went Wrong?" *Survival*, Autumn 2001.
Romesh Ratnesar	"To the Brink," *Time*, March 4, 2002.
Sara Roy	"Why Peace Failed: An Oslo Autopsy," *Current History*, January 2002.
Eric Rozenman	"Today's Arab Israelis, Tomorrow's Israel," *Policy Review*, April/May 2001.
David Schafer	"Origins of the Israeli-Palestinian Conflict," *Humanist*, July/August 2002.
Ze'ev Schiff	"The Ubiquitous Palestinian Question," *World Press Review*, January 2002.
Mark Silverberg	"Only Resolve Is Respected," *Midstream*, February/March 2003.
Joshua Sinai	"Intifada Drives Both Sides (Israelis and Palestinians) to Radical Arms," *Jane's Intelligence Review*, May 2001.
Saul Singer	"Paradigms for a Mideast Peace," *New Leader*, March/April 2002.
Sandra S. Tamari	"Ariel Sharon's 'War Against Terror' Is a War Against All Palestinians," *Synthesis/Regeneration*, Fall 2002.
Stuart Taylor	"Opening Argument—Civilized People View the Killing of Innocent Civilians as Abhorrent. Unfortunately, in the Israel-Palestinian Conflict, Many Muslims and Arabs See It as a Means to an End," *National Journal*, 2002.
Shibley Telhami	"Why Suicide Terrorism Takes Root," *New York Times*, April 4, 2002.
Graham Usher	"Palestine: Ending the Illusion," *Middle East International*, April 19, 2002.
Alison Weir	"Is Israel Poised for a New Round of Ethnic Cleansing?" *Washington Report on Middle East Affairs*, April 2003.
Sherwin Wine	"Arabs and Jews," *Humanist*, September/October 2002.
Mortimer Zuckerman	"Arafat Must Be Stopped," *U.S. News & World Report*, September 29, 2003.

Index

problems with, 18–19, 37–39
proposed, 9
road map to peace, 10, 37–39, 52
Peres, Shimon, 48
pogroms, 8–9
preemptive policy, 42–44
Proxmire amendment, 30

Qalqilya, 65–66
Queri, Ahmed, 10

Rabin, Yitzhak, 47, 48, 54, 59
Rajoub, Jibril, 41
road map to peace, 10, 37–39, 52
Rozenman, Eric L., 51
Rumsfeld, Donald, 43

Sadat, Anwar, 9
Saramago, Jose, 16
Saudi Arabia
  diplomacy of, 25–26
  U.S. military bases in, 31
security wall
  benefits of, 61–62
  is necessary, 58–62
  will harm Palestinians, 63–66
September 11, 2001, aftermath of, 8
Shahin, Mariam, 63
Sharon, Ariel
  Jewish settlements added by, 13
  peace initiatives and, 49, 50
  power of, 17–18
  response of, to Netanya bombing, 8
  on war on terrorism, 8
Singer, Joel, 20
Six Day War, 9, 30
Students for Justice in Palestine, 32
suicide bombings, 8, 9, 15–16
SUSTAIN, 32
Syria, 26

terrorism
  ending peace talks and, 8, 9
  Palestinian Authority supports, 40–42
  preemptive attacks against, are the
    only solution, 42–44
  security wall is necessary against,

58–62
terrorist groups, 9
two-state solution
  Bush and, 26, 45, 51–52
  is flawed, 51–57
  is needed, 45–50
  no room for, 56

Unger, David C., 45
UN Global Conference Against Racism,
  32
United Nations
  Israeli-Palestinian conflict and, 12
  Resolution 181, 20
  Resolution 194, 21, 25
  Resolution 242, 22, 54, 56
  Resolution 338, 54
United States
  Israeli lobby in, 12
  oil interests of, 30–31
  relationship between Israel and, 30–33
  war on terrorism by, 8
U.S. aid
  enhances Israeli security, 35–36
  enhances U.S. security, 34–35
  has worsened conflict, 28–33
  is helping resolve Israeli-Palestinian
    conflict, 34–36
U.S. Foreign Assistance Act, 30
U.S. foreign policy, 30–31

war on terrorism
  after September 11, 2001, 8
  U.S. aid to Israel and, 34–35
West Bank
  Jewish settlements in, 11–12
  security wall in, 63–65
Wieseltier, Leon, 14

Ya'alon, Moshe, 39
Yom Kippur War, 54

Zahran, Marouf, 66
Zinni, Anthony, 41, 50
Zuckerman, Mortimer B., 40
Zunes, Stephen, 30
Zur, Ofer, 58